"This masterwork blazes with Elijah-fire yet flows with calm wisdom. Through crystalline prose and prophetic insight, Dr. Chironna guides us to hear God in the whispers, not just the whirlwinds. This is what prophetic formation looks like—where discernment meets devotion and listening births legacy. A balm in Gilead and a bomb in Babylon for those willing to 'slow down to the speed of revelation' (a phrase worth the book's price)."

Leonard Sweet, professor; preacher; publisher; proprietor, Sanctuary Seaside, Orcas Island, Washington; author, *Decoding the Divine*

"Voices! So many loud and diverse voices make discernment difficult and biblical understanding confusing at best. But my longtime friend Dr. Mark Chironna is at his best in *Prophetic Integrity and the Elijah Legacy*, where in quintessential Chironna communication he leads us through the life and times of Elijah to make the ancient contemporary. You'll want to share this book with all new and seasoned believers."

Sam Chand, leadership consultant

"Chironna invites readers into a contemplative reading of the story of Elijah to deepen their union and communion with God. Prophetic consciousness emerges from a silent listening and meditative discerning in the presence of the triune God. Weaving together insights from Christian tradition and contemporary psychology, Chironna suggests that the path to the prophetic is through the sanctifying work of spiritual formation. Reading this book is a journey through the human heart into the heart of God. I warmly recommend it."

Dale M. Coulter, DPhil, Robert E. Fisher Chair of Spiritual Renewal and professor of historical theology, Pentecostal Theological Seminary

"*Prophetic Integrity and the Elijah Legacy* is that rare devotional work that is challenging without being harsh or heavy, uplifting without being formulaic. Chironna does not shy away from the reality of false prophets and corrupt authorities, and he does not shrink back from the ugly truths of Elijah's inner conflict. Inst~~ ~~ reading of the text, he allows the Scri this time of fear and uncertainty, call

identity as the people of God and drawing us out into the deeper currents of the Spirit. Above all, this book reminds us that prophetic integrity is not found in easy assurances or displays of power but in the patience and compassion learned by abiding in the sufferings of Christ."

Chris E. W. Green, bishop ordinary, Diocese of St. Anthony; professor of public theology, Southeastern University

"*Prophetic Integrity and the Elijah Legacy* is a call to prophetic faithfulness wherein Dr. Mark Chironna draws on decades of prophetic experience and scholarship. It addresses the challenges we face in living out our callings with integrity. I've been waiting for a book like this to add to my library."

Chris Palmer, PhD, dean and associate professor, Barnett College of Ministry and Theology, Southeastern University

"Dr. Mark Chironna has the unique combination of a brilliant intellect and a mature spirituality sharpened over half a century of ministry experience. This makes him a formidable individual. Despite this academic prowess, he writes in an incredibly accessible way. Like they said of Jesus, 'The common people heard him gladly.' I have no doubt this will become a rich resource for many."

Peter Prothero, senior pastor, Equippers Bristol

"Dr. Chironna is highly respected and a favorite on GOD TV and has impacted countless lives around the world. This book is powerful, passionate, and provoking, filled with Scripture, personal experiences, and profound insights. It is accessible, deeply enriching, and clearly a culmination of a lifetime of walking with Christ."

Ward Simpson, president, GOD TV

PROPHETIC INTEGRITY
AND THE
ELIJAH LEGACY

BOOKS BY MARK CHIRONNA

On the Edge of Hope
Rising with Hope
Prophetic Integrity and the Elijah Legacy

PROPHETIC INTEGRITY AND THE ELIJAH LEGACY

CULTIVATING A LISTENING EAR
AND A DISCERNING HEART

MARK CHIRONNA

Chosen

a division of Baker Publishing Group
Minneapolis, Minnesota

© 2025 by Dr. Mark Chironna

Published by Chosen Books
Minneapolis, Minnesota
ChosenBooks.com

Chosen Books is a division of
Baker Publishing Group, Grand Rapids, Michigan

Printed in the United States of America

All rights reserved. No part of this publication may be reproduced, stored in a retrieval system, or transmitted in any form or by any means—for example, electronic, photocopy, recording—without the prior written permission of the publisher. The only exception is brief quotations in printed reviews.

Library of Congress Cataloging-in-Publication Data
Names: Chironna, Mark, author.
Title: Prophetic integrity and the Elijah legacy : cultivating a listening ear and a discerning heart / Dr. Mark Chironna.
Description: Minneapolis, Minnesota : Chosen, a division of Baker Publishing Group, [2025] | Includes bibliographical references.
Identifiers: LCCN 2024035939 | ISBN 9780800773113 (paperback) | ISBN 9780800773182 (casebound) | ISBN 9781493450497 (ebook)
Subjects: LCSH: Elijah (Biblical prophet) | Elisha (Biblical prophet) | Prophecy—Christianity—Biblical teaching.
Classification: LCC BS580.E4 C45 2025 | DDC 222/.50922—dc23/eng/20250108
LC record available at https://lccn.loc.gov/2024035939

Unless otherwise indicated, Scripture quotations are from the New Revised Standard Version Bible, copyright © 1989 National Council of the Churches of Christ in the United States of America. Used by permission. All rights reserved worldwide.

Scripture quotations identified KJV are from the King James Version of the Bible.

Scripture quotations identified LSB taken from the (LSB®) Legacy Standard Bible®, Copyright © 2021 by The Lockman Foundation. Used by permission. All rights reserved. Managed in partnership with Three Sixteen Publishing Inc. LSBible.org and 316publishing.com.

Scripture quotations marked LEB are from the *Lexham English Bible.* Copyright 2012 Logos Bible Software. Lexham is a registered trademark of Logos Bible Software.

Scripture quotations identified NASB taken from the (NASB®) New American Standard Bible®, Copyright © 1960, 1971, 1977, 1995 by The Lockman Foundation. Used by permission. All rights reserved. www.lockman.org

Scripture identified NKJV taken from the New King James Version®. Copyright © 1982 by Thomas Nelson. Used by permission. All rights reserved.

Cover design by Peter Gloege, Look Design Studio

Baker Publishing Group publications use paper produced from sustainable forestry practices and postconsumer waste whenever possible.

25 26 27 28 29 30 31   7 6 5 4 3 2 1

To my beloved wife, Ruth—Your unwavering love, grace, and support have made this work possible. Thank you for your willingness to allow me the time and space to pursue the calling God has placed on my life, including the hours invested in writing this book. Your patience and encouragement have been a constant source of strength, and your selflessness in making room for this endeavor is a gift I treasure. This book is as much a reflection of your love as it is of my labor. With all my heart, I thank you.

CONTENTS

Foreword by Bishop Tudor Bismark 11
Introduction 13

1. Knowing Where We Come From 21
2. Elijah the Larger-Than-Life Prophet 37
3. Journeying with Elijah: The Tishbite and His Call 47
4. Look What the Wind Blew In (to Ahab's Court) 65
5. Knowing Where We're Going 73
6. Fed by Dirty Birds 89
7. Life in a Culture of Death 109
8. On the Threshold of Flourishing 127
9. Rising out of Dead Things 137
10. The Hour Has Come 153
11. Place Your Bets 163
12. Restoring the Altar of the Lord 181
13. Is It Rain That I Hear? 195

Not-So-Final Thoughts 211
Acknowledgments 213
Notes 215

FOREWORD

It is known and frequently discussed that there is a leadership deficit in the world. More so in the Body of Christ. It has become necessary to address these empty spaces. Of the many books written on leadership, very few, if any, adequately address leadership from an apostolic and prophetic perspective. Even fewer of those books reach the depth of apostolic and prophetic ministry Dr. Mark Chironna has.

Dr. Chironna has produced a classic. It is said that many things are caught and not taught. It is needful that this book is both caught and taught. Major deficits in the global Body of Christ have not been addressed adequately. So God must, every now and then, elevate an individual to speak intellectually, academically, apostolically, and prophetically into the vacuum.

Dr. Chironna has over fifty years of ministry and leadership experience, and God has blessed him to be amphibious (that is, flourishing in many worlds) and well received. He has a record of faithfully following those who have gone before; relating to peers with honesty, openness, and integrity; and mentoring many younger than he. He has mastered the ability to effectively communicate what he has heard from God.

In this magnificent manuscript, he has boldly addressed the void that exists both secularly and spiritually. This book defines

Foreword

the principle of going through a process, exhuming the chronological order of the evolution of a person, a prophet, a place, a people, and a purpose. Many don't want the process, resist the process, despise the process, and therefore never evolve into a dynamic entity capable of disrupting disorder while at the same time introducing, developing, and maintaining order.

There's always a basic way to do something, but Dr. Chironna offers a guide and recommendation for a more excellent way. This book is a discovery of the better way in which God wants to establish His will, His purposes, and His leaders on earth.

Not all who say they are apostles are apostles, and not all who say they are prophets are prophets. Many function in those self-proclaimed roles without process, rank, order, or accountability, and do not submit to a leader or a system that can bring direction and correction.

Something in the heavenly realm is moving as creation is groaning, anticipating the manifestation of the sons of God. This new era—what the prophets prophesied, what Jesus predicted—is upon us. We are blessed to have Dr. Chironna present this well-done treatise to propel us forward into renewed tenets of faith, including the art of humility, the act of wildness, the spirit of integrity, and the grace of honor necessary for what God is about to do.

As a student, an observer, or simply a curious reader, open your heart, your spirit, your mind to the truth spelled out here. Ask the Holy Spirit to open your eyes and ears of understanding so that you can receive an impartation of this jubilee work. This is a work of liberation, restoration, and all things new.

God bless Dr. Chironna for this outstanding work.

Bishop Tudor Bismark, Harare, Zimbabwe

INTRODUCTION

It has taken me fifty years to write this book—fifty years of meditating on the Scriptures and living through challenges, moments of insight, and experiences of breakthrough. My hope is that you will think of these pages as a personal conversation between us. You might notice that, although I don't always say it plainly, I often share with you from a place of self-disclosure—not only of my highs and lows but also of my hunger for intimacy with the God we know as Father, Son, and Spirit.

Because my life in the sacred text is inseparable from my life overall, I've poured into these pages scriptural insights and reflections. Many of them are tied to the life of Elijah, a man of passions and limitations who learned to tune in to God's communications, even when they came through the slightest whispers of creation. Such elements were his first teachers in the art of listening, and they shaped his prophetic voice. You could say he developed a quality of attention essential to one's relationship with God.

I believe this type of focused attention was what Saint Paul referred to when he instructed the Thessalonians to "pray without ceasing" (1 Thessalonians 5:17). Elijah's focus sensitized him and prepared him to encounter God not only in the

Introduction

dramatic phenomena of wind, earthquake, or fire but in the sheer silence on Mount Horeb. Elijah discerned God in the silence and recognized His presence in a still, small voice.

In keeping with the themes of listening and discerning, Elijah's life challenges us to engage deeply with Scripture and with the community of believers. The mandate to avoid "private interpretations" emphasizes this communal aspect of faith. As Peter warned, "No prophecy of scripture is a matter of one's own interpretation, because no prophecy ever came by human will, but men and women moved by the Holy Spirit spoke from God" (2 Peter 1:20–21). We are to seek wisdom collectively, grounded in the Tradition, "the faith that was once for all entrusted to the saints" (Jude 3). As Jaroslav Pelikan beautifully explained, Tradition is the "living faith of the dead; traditionalism is the dead faith of the living."[1]

This book therefore focuses on the ancient faith and the tried-and-true practices that help us to become fully immersed in communion with God. Through deep listening, stillness, silence, and beholding, we can see the living faith of the dead come alive in us. This will certainly be true as we explore certain narratives from the sacred text. Over the decades, I have wrestled with them to the point that not only have I read them, but they have read me. In my walk with Jesus, I have learned He fully intends for this to happen, by the Spirit, as often as we give Him our attention.

Slowing Down in a Too-Fast World

Two favorite expressions are ones I share often with our church family: "Slow down to the speed of life" and "Slow down to the speed of revelation." The idea of slowing down goes back to my youth and a song Chuck Girard wrote entitled "Slow Down."[2] Love Song sang it, and it became an anthem for people like me who were swept into the kingdom during the Jesus People

Introduction

Movement. We were troubled by the turbulence of the 1960s and early '70s. Our generation found fault with many things, and we needed hope and space to breathe. We needed to slow down from the dizzying speed of change in the world. That was then. Today's pace of change makes those years seem almost peaceful by comparison! The alarming rise in depression, anxieties, and trauma-related issues, along with broader concerns of mental illness, is staggering and well-documented. Because this reality affects our listening as Jesus summons us into the future, I need to substantiate these claims with actual data:

- A comprehensive study conducted from 2005 to 2018 by Johns Hopkins Bloomberg School of Public Health and Columbia University reveals a significant increase in mental health issues among adolescents. Utilizing data from more than 200,000 adolescents, the study showed not only a rise in those seeking treatment or counseling for mental health problems but also a notable increase in "'internalizing' problems" such as "anxiety, depression, and suicidal thoughts."[3] Particularly alarming is the sharp rise in suicidal thoughts or attempts, with an increase by 63.3 percent during the study period.[4]
- *Psychology Today* highlights the global escalation in anxiety and depression during the COVID-19 pandemic, with prevalence among girls and young women increasing markedly and attributed in part to the impact of social media.[5] This source also indicates a persistent upward trend involving depressive and anxiety disorders, with no declines since measurements began in 1990—despite the availability of more support services and interventions.[6]
- In the five years prior to the pandemic, increasing anxiety and depression were evident among children

Introduction

between the ages of three and seventeen. And by 2020—before the pandemic exacerbated these issues—millions of children had been diagnosed with these conditions. College students are not immune to deteriorating mental health. More than 60 percent faced "at least one mental health problem" during the first full school year during the pandemic.[7] This indicates a widespread mental health crisis among students, exacerbated by the pandemic but rooted in deeper, systemic issues.[8]

- These issues are not limited to our youth. The stats revealing mental health challenges among adults are also staggering. In fact, 22.8 percent of adults in the United States were reported to have mental health issues.[9] That is almost one-quarter of our adult population.

These statistics are sobering reminders of the profound brokenness and dysfunction present in our "advanced" society. I wish I could say these data don't include people who love and follow Jesus. But after many decades in the people-helping field, I know that's not true. People in the church of Jesus Christ are also suffering with mental health challenges. Our involvement with social media narratives is not helping. Too many of us are caught up in memes that mask the truth, sow more discord than understanding, and wear us down emotionally. Before we claim "God said" this or "God said" that, let's be sure our actions (or inactions) do not overlook the deep trauma and heartache experienced by so many all around us.

Obviously, the COVID-19 pandemic didn't help our mental health. Although it seemed to slow us down, it also increased stress and left physical, emotional, and spiritual scars for countless thousands upon thousands of people who are still navigating a difficult path toward healing. And that doesn't include all the other traumas that plague our generation. If we are willing to learn anything from history (which is something our

Introduction

postmodern culture has seduced many into rejecting), it is this: Our little blue planet's history is filled with stories of Christian communities in every nation overcoming great adversities, traumas, plagues, atrocities, and violence. They did it by coming together, leaning on faith, and extending a helping hand to those in need.

Now is the time for us to do the same—to look beyond our differences and allow the common ground of our humanity to unite us. If we are striving to listen and discern but are not hearing about being committed vessels of God's love and compassion, are we really listening to the Holy Spirit?

Three Questions

The statistics and insights I just shared remind us our wellbeing is fragile. Does the Spirit have anything to say through His people from a therapeutic perspective? We cannot give to others what we ourselves do not have. So as Christ's brothers and sisters, perhaps we first need to embrace His therapeutic, healing presence and hear His word to us as "healing word" so we can share it with others.

We need to ask ourselves why we listen to what Jesus speaks to us personally and collectively. Is it so we can feel spiritually advanced? Will we use it to drive issues and divide our ranks over popular but suspect interpretations of Scripture? Of course not! What if Jesus is calling us to walk in the fellowship of His sufferings so we can truly know the power of His resurrection? What if *that* path is the way to understanding, empathy, and redemptive action?

A deeply personal experience might help to explain the matter of listening, discerning, and stepping forward in faith. As I shared in my book *On the Edge of Hope*, I emerged from a prolonged, traumatic period of darkness and questioning in 2010 with three crucial questions that continue to shape my

Introduction

journey. These questions—What is Jesus up to? Where is He going? Am I going with Him?—are not rhetorical. Hour by hour, they direct me through the complexities of faith and existence, as a child of God and as a spiritual leader in the Body of Christ. They are a guiding light that prompts my pursuit of understanding the times, knowing what to do, and knowing what steps to take (1 Chronicles 12:32).

These questions are intertwined with the practice of deep listening to the indwelling Spirit. This pursuit of clarity and purpose is especially important in our fast-paced world, where distractions abound and silence is scarce. The current barrage of information and demands can muddle our ability to discern the Lord's subtle movements and messages. It's like trying to hear a gentle melody in the middle of a cacophony. Unless we deliberately filter out the noise and attune ourselves to the quieter sounds, the melody's essence is obscured or even lost to us.

Growing–Together

One of the "quieter sounds" we tend to miss is the idea that the church is a body. We tend to focus on our growth as individuals, but what about our development as a community? The transition from a deeply personal quest to a broader contemplation of our collective spiritual journey is essential and underscores the universal challenge of seeking divine guidance and presence in the tumult of everyday life. As we journey together, we are drawn into a posture of intentional slowness. Then the idea of slowing down to the speed of life and revelation isn't merely poetic. It's a deep, life-changing practice that prods us to purge the distractions that besiege us. It calls us to resist mental shortcuts that bypass the richness of contemplation. It quiets the mental chatter that often masquerades as engagement with truth.

The Scriptures are truly God-breathed, offering us a wellspring of divine wisdom and revelation. Yet our desires, biases,

Introduction

and frenetic thought-lives and schedules can cloud our approach to Scripture. Instead of listening attentively to what the text actually says, we find ourselves reading into it what we want to hear. The distinction is subtle but substantial. Our misreading of Scripture, however unwitting it might be, can lead us far from the intention and heart of God.

When we slow down and acknowledge this error, we realize the importance of not just reading the Scriptures but truly listening and allowing their truth to seep into our beings. This requires an openness to being taught, corrected, and guided by the Word. It means resisting any temptation to bend the text and make it fit our preconceived notions. It's about coming to the Scriptures with humility, ready to hear and accept the revelation they contain, even when it challenges us.

Let's face it. If I cannot hear the voice of Jesus, by the Spirit, in the sacred text, I will never discern His voice within the context of my everyday life. So I must learn in the Scriptures and as I walk the path before me to ask, "What is Jesus up to? Where is He going? Am I going with Him?"

Listening to Discern—Discerning to Step Forward

Listening deeply to God is the cornerstone of everything we will explore together. Elijah's life exemplifies the practices of listening deeply and discerning wisely in a noisy world. His journey serves as a blueprint, not for replicating his calling or unique way of life, but for attuning our hearts to hear God's voice.

Listening is about more than capturing stray thoughts during prayer. It means cultivating a practice of stillness where true listening can occur. Imagine it as creating a sacred space where every distracting noise fades away, and God's voice becomes clear and discernible. This practice of listening is a journey to understanding that God's whispers are often found in the silence we create, a silence that invites us to hear with our hearts.

Introduction

As we will soon see, discernment is the pathway through the forest of our thoughts, emotions, and the divergent voices that clamor for our attention. Drawing from the Christian Tradition, we will explore how to sift through what we hear, separate out the chaff, and align our hearts with God's heart. It is a journey to recognizing God's ways of speaking to us. The aim is to help us distinguish His voice from the noise and understand how that enriches our lives.

Listening and discerning are essential practices that enable us to step forward by faith. It means taking what we have heard and discerned and weaving it into the fabric of our lives. We take each step forward knowing that even when we don't see the entire path, we can trust in the One who is guiding us. It's about moving with intention in the strength of our faith and in the direction of what we discern, even when one step is all we can see.

We are being invited to engage with our individual spiritual journeys in ways that are grounded in the collective wisdom of the faith. Let's remember that we stand on the shoulders of giants—the sages, saints, and scholars who have walked this path before us. Their lives, reflections, and interpretations offer invaluable insights into the heart of God as revealed in Scripture, the Tradition, and the wisdom of our spiritual ancestors. To overlook this guidance is to forfeit treasuries of enlightenment that can expand our understanding and deepen our faith. Our ancestors' stories are rich with divine encounters and human frailty, and they offer us timeless lessons on how to navigate our own spiritual journeys.

So whether you're seeking guidance, inspiration, or a deeper understanding of how to hear from God in a complex world, let's embark on this journey, not just as author and reader but as fellow travelers navigating our spiritual lives with intention, courage, and faith.

1

Knowing Where We Come From

Hear, O Israel: the LORD our God, the LORD is one!

Deuteronomy 6:4 NKJV

As the saying goes, if you don't know where you come from, you won't know where you're going. A big part of knowing where we come from is understanding where we are in relation to history. Our hearts seem naturally drawn to Scripture's ancient stories. Their relevance is timeless and reminds us our world is filled with mystery and wonder, miracles, and majesty. They awaken us from a deepening sleep and state of fragmentation to a restored sense of enchantment that Hollywood could never author.

From a Disenchanted World

A certain truth about our world is undeniable. It is heavy with disenchantment and crying out for healing. This condition touches a nerve with us. It ignites an innate plea to rediscover the connection that once animated the human spirit with wonder and respect for the mysteries all around us. Prior to the Enlightenment, beginning in the late seventeenth century, atheists were a rarity. But since the Enlightenment crowned rationalism as its king, the human race has become progressively disenchanted. Many people have relinquished the religious and spiritual beliefs that permeated everyday life when virtually everyone believed in some form of divine presence. Without such an ethos, the world can only settle for the limits of human reason.

The Enlightenment's emphasis on reason and empirical evidence fundamentally challenged traditional religious views and opened the door to a broader spectrum of beliefs, including atheism. Its effects continue; in the early twentieth century, philosopher Max Weber stated, "The fate of our times is characterized by rationalization and intellectualization and, above all, by the 'disenchantment of the world.'"[1] This push for everything to be more logical comes at a cost. As Weber warned, the disenchantment that keeps us focused on facts and efficiency also obscures the sense of wonder and mystery that once colored humanity's understanding of life. He urges us to pause and consider what we leave behind when we prioritize the practical over the magical.

Philosopher Charles Taylor builds on Weber's insights and considers the consequences of the shift toward rationality. In his book *A Secular Age*, Taylor references Weber's ideas and meticulously traces the evolution from a world of unquestioned belief in God to our current era, in which spirituality is one option among many. He describes how people once saw themselves inhabiting a world filled with spirits and unseen forces—a premodern perspective he calls the "porous self."[2]

In science, *porous* implies something that allows liquids or gases to pass through it.[3] Taylor uses the term to describe a self that is open to and influenced by unseen spiritual forces and

Knowing Where We Come From

feels connected to a world beyond what is strictly physical. This was the pre-Enlightenment norm. Historically, the thought of relying solely on human logic and rejecting all things supernatural was foreign, because people believed without question that spiritual influences inhabited the world.

However, as science progressed, it dismissed these mystical elements. Instead of the porous self, there was now what Taylor calls the "buffered self," which is separated from mystical forces.[4] In science, *buffering* means adding substances to solutions in order to stabilize pH levels.[5] Taylor applies the concept to Enlightenment perspectives, with the buffered self being protected from external forces, particularly unseen ones.

From this perspective, reason and knowledge make the world legible and manageable. Taylor notes that when science replaced the mystical, we learned to sort out moral and existential questions without seeking God-centered explanations. We essentially declared our independence from God, much as Adam and Eve did at the Tree of the Knowledge of Good and Evil. In transitioning from the porous self (and society) to a buffered self (and society), we became more thoroughly individualistic and secular. Now, centuries after these shifts began, they continue shaping our concepts of faith and meaning.

From Spiritual Sleep

Where does this way of being leave us? Simply put, we are caught in the currents of a cultural river, inheriting generations of thought patterns, often without realizing it. Even if we have deep faith in Christ, we aren't immune to these currents. All of us are influenced in subtle ways, and much of it happens without our conscious awareness.

As we tackle today's problems, we tend to seek quick solutions and mental shortcuts. Although we believe we are listening and discerning, the influences that shape our thoughts and psyches are operating undercover and escaping our notice. We need the Spirit's guidance to search our hearts and reveal how we've been buffered (to use Taylor's term). However, the layers of this effect can obscure our view and conceal the spiritual battles in play—battles with unseen forces that have real impacts.

The apostle Paul warned us about the things we fail to see and cautioned us against living on autopilot. This oblivious way of life is possible because we are asleep when we should be awake. This sleep state prevents us from seizing the moment for the glory of God. It is only when we are awake and listening deeply that we are able to consciously commune with the Lord. Please read Paul's warning slowly—and I do mean *slowly*:

> Let no one deceive you with empty words, for because of these things the wrath of God comes on those who are disobedient. Therefore do not be associated with them. For once you were darkness, but now in the Lord you are light. Live as children of light—for the fruit of the light is found in all that is good and right and true. Try to find out what is pleasing to the Lord. Take no part in the unfruitful works of darkness, but instead expose them. For it is shameful even to mention what such people do secretly; but everything exposed by the light becomes visible, for everything that becomes visible is light. Therefore it says, "Sleeper, awake! Rise from the dead, and Christ will shine on you."
>
> Be careful then how you live, not as unwise people but as wise, making the most of the time, because the days are evil.
>
> Ephesians 5:6–16

Paul's metaphor of waking up and letting Christ shine on us evoked for Ephesian believers the Old Testament imagery of *theophany*, a manifestation of God's presence that brings light and revelation. The idea of awakening and arising suggests a transition from darkness to light, symbolizing spiritual renewal and enlightenment that are transformative. Paul called

Knowing Where We Come From

the Ephesians and us to leave behind the behaviors and patterns of a metaphorically dead life that is disconnected from God's truth and wisdom. This arising from the dead suggests resurrection—not just in the eschatological sense, but as a present and active revival of the spiritual life.

The idea that Christ will shine on you is a prophetic reminder of momentous Old Testament occasions when God's appearance brought light to dark situations. Do you remember when Moses descended from Mount Sinai, his face aglow with God's glory? What about the majestic sight of Elijah being swept up into the heavens in a fiery chariot, and Isaiah's exultation, "Arise, shine; for your light has come, and the glory of the LORD has risen upon you"? (See Exodus 34:29; 2 Kings 2:11–12; Isaiah 60:1.)

Saint Paul beckons us to transcend our past limitations, not through our power, but through the indwelling life of the ascended Christ. Paul's instruction to "be careful . . . how you live, not as unwise people but as wise, making the most of the time, because the days are evil" underscores our need to be awake and conduct ourselves with vigilance and discernment, particularly in times of spiritual and moral complexity (Ephesians 5:15–16). The New King James Version of this passage speaks of "redeeming the time" (v. 16). In other words, we are to live wisely and seize every moment, living in *kairos* (or God's time, which we will discuss later) and manifesting Christ's light in a spiritually darkened world.

Paul's ancient counsel resonates today. The early or primitive church was not rudimentary or backward. The word *primitive* refers to the church's essential nature as a vibrant community alive in the Spirit. As people of the Spirit, we aspire to emulate the early church, challenging the assumption that *newer* means *better*. In reality, ancient wisdom often holds the key to navigating our present. So I often say, "Out with the old, and in with the older!"

Absolutes are questioned in our postmodern setting, and truth seems elusive. Disenchantment is more than the fading of fairy tales and magical thinking; it is a painful disorientation and detachment from the mysterious threads that weave the earthly with the heavenly. As a culture, we are losing touch with the divine essence that underpins and unites all aspects of existence. As the sacred becomes increasingly obscured, we fall into a deepening spiritual sleep.

From a Place of Fragmentation

God intends for us to possess a prophetic and visionary sense that guides us toward His desired destiny for us. This sense comes from Jesus calling us toward the greater future He inhabits, and it safeguards us against the fragmentation and disintegration surrounding us. On the path to healing and sanctification, each of us embodies brokenness and beauty. The journey toward wholeness addresses the fragmentation caused by the wounds we have suffered. Healing reintegrates us, producing a sense of wholeness and internal integrity.

A prophetic vision is critical to our internal cohesion (Proverbs 29:18), our spiritual and emotional well-being, and an integrated identity. A lack of internal integrity disintegrates the *self*. An offhand approach to prophetic revelation only adds to this condition. Too often, the term *prophetic revelation* is used to label and falsely validate someone's personal insights. Frequently, these insights do not square with Scripture or the Tradition; yet they are said to carry divine authority. This is a claim that ought never to be issued or received lightly.

This issue exposes the fragmentation it means to address. Fragmentation is more prevalent than we'd like to admit, and it signals the need for reform. Recognizing and validating spiritual insights is a serious issue. I raise it here in hopes of encouraging an authentic understanding of prophetic revelation as defined in Scripture and upheld by the great theologians of the church. Therefore, I propose a practice of listening, discerning, and acting that is reverent toward Christ and acknowledges the weightiness of claiming to speak on God's behalf. The re-anchoring of genuine prophetic revelation means owning the broader task of finding meaning and connection in a disenchanted and despairing world. Re-enchantment requires us to actively engage and deepen our intimacy with both the triune God and the human experience. Exploring arts and literature that reflect the human condition can help us; but an intentional focus on the ancient faith and its proven practices of deep listening, stillness, silence, and beholding will immerse us in what is most important—our communion with God.

Toward Re-enchantment

The "out with the old and in with the older" approach I mentioned makes room for re-enchantment based in deep intimacy with the Father, the Son, and the Spirit. From that posture, we can live in what Pentecostal scholar and prophetic mentor Rickie D. Moore refers to as the "Pentecost Spirit," which transcends denominational lines and forms us in the image and likeness of Jesus.

Living this way does not require us to abandon rational thought. It simply notes logic is but one facet of engaging with our world. The journey toward re-enchantment will not only enrich our personal lives but also bring us closer to the true essence of prophetic revelation. That in turn calls us to a deeper, more holistic understanding of our place in the cosmos. It is not necessary to turn back the clock to simpler times or deny the advances we have made. I suggest it starts simply by nurturing our own curiosity, cultivating wonder, and embracing the mysteries inherent in our communion with God.

Communing with the God who is communion in His very being helps us to become visionary again. Instead of being bound by rationalism, we are called to see the unseen, hear the unheard, and speak the unspoken. In a world that is rushing forward, being re-enchanted means noticing the miraculous in the mundane. It can be as simple as seeing the wonders of creation in a fallen leaf.

This personal re-enchantment can ripple outward, influencing our interaction with others and our care for our world. We might even discover that the healing we seek for our planet begins in our lived experiences. It involves the deliberate reinvigoration of our capacity to see the extraordinary in the ordinary. It requires something I mentioned earlier—slowing down to the speed of life and revelation.

Solomon said that without prophetic revelation, our lives disintegrate. The Lexham English Bible translates Solomon's statement this way: "When there is no prophecy, the people cast off restraint" (Proverbs 29:18 LEB). *Prophecy* can refer to "vision" and "often refers specifically to prophetic vision or divine revelation."[6] This divine revelation—or *prophetic revelation*—implies God-given insight or understanding rather than personal ambition or foresight. When Solomon speaks of "casting off restraint," the Hebrew word is פָּרַע (*para*), commonly interpreted "to be out of control."[7] This implies a breakdown of moral, social, or spiritual order, common in the absence of moral guidance and divine direction. In other words, our moral compass gives way. Personal and societal chaos ensue, and we find ourselves desperately needing the moral, God-ordained enchantment that once was.

Re-enchantment and Listening

So how do we get re-enchanted while living in a disenchanted culture? I believe it is by hearing the Spirit's clarion call to deep listening. The words "Hear, O Israel" from Deuteronomy 6:4 beckon

Knowing Where We Come From

us not only to hear but to truly listen. At one level, the physical experience of hearing is the passive way in which our senses acknowledge sound. Listening, however, requires active engagement, a deliberate act of drawing closer to what is being communicated. When Scripture uses the word *hear* in Deuteronomy 6:4 and elsewhere, it is not about passively receiving sound. The Hebrew word *shema* is often translated "hear," but it implies the deep and active listening that demands our full engagement. We are not only to internalize the message but to respond via our actions. This kind of hearing is inseparable from the ancient practice of communion with God and involves not only the mind but also the heart and soul.

This kind of listening is integral to the spiritual life. It attunes us to the divine voice, freeing us to discern God's will and align our lives with His life and commands. Deep listening inclines us to respond with commitment and devotion. This is a sacred act that begins by divine invitation. Often in the narrative of Israel, God's people turned their backs on this conversation with Yahweh and became spiritually deaf. They abandoned the Shema, the most important prayer of their faith, and turned to false narratives and "dumb idols" (1 Corinthians 12:2 NKJV). Their story reminds us that when we are unwilling to listen, we become unable to speak.

Prophetic Consciousness as Sacred Exchange

Certain monumental figures stand against the backdrop of spiritual decline. They are the prophets who teach us the critical importance of attentiveness. The late rabbi and philosopher-theologian Abraham Joshua Heschel highlighted the prophets' ability to perceive God's heart and respond to His call, writing,

Prophecy consists in the inspired communication of divine attitudes to the prophetic consciousness. The divine pathos is the ground-tone of all these attitudes. Echoed in almost every prophetic statement, pathos is the central category of the prophetic understanding of God.[8]

Prophetic consciousness is about more than predicting future events or voicing divine decrees; it is a sacred exchange by which God's deepest yearnings infuse the prophet's own heart, and ultimately our hearts, as God's children. Prophetic consciousness works with our everyday, human consciousness. Philosopher and psychologist William James describes the latter as a continuous flow, much like a river in which thoughts and perceptions stream one after the other, seamlessly. Here is how James describes the ever-changing fluidity of our human consciousness:

> Consciousness, then, does not appear to itself chopped up in bits. Such words as "chain" or "train" do not describe it fitly as it presents itself in the first instance. It is nothing jointed; it flows. A "river" or a "stream" are the metaphors by which it is most naturally described. In talking of it hereafter, let us call it the stream of thought, of consciousness, or of subjective life.[9]

For James, consciousness isn't comprised of disconnected fragments that are strung together. It is fluid and continuous, so our thoughts and perceptions are not isolated but seamlessly linked. By referring to "stream of thought . . . consciousness, or of subjective life,"[10] James suggests not a static mental life but one in which thoughts, feelings, and perceptions continuously merge and influence one another.

Prophetic Consciousness and the City of God

Consider the beautiful imagery of Psalm 46:4. "There is a river whose streams make glad the city of God, the holy habitation of the Most High." The sons of Korah paint a picture here of God's city being enriched and enlivened by a river with many streams. This motif echoes the river in Eden that branched into four life-giving rivers (Genesis 2:10–14).

Psalm 46 takes me back to my Bible school days and my dear late friend, mentor, and teacher, Vinnie. His way of engaging with God was enchanting. Whenever he prayed, praised, or worshiped, my desire for a deeper connection with God increased. Vinnie was profoundly attuned to the flow of the River of God—the Holy Spirit. His teachings frequently returned to the scriptural city of God, which for Vinnie was not about a heavenly future but a present reality within us.

Vinnie envisioned each of us as a temple of the Holy Spirit with the River flowing from our innermost being. He lived with the constant awareness of the divine flow that sustains each believer's "inner city." Vinnie often taught on the psalms of the sons of Korah and about how they address the ways our rebellion against God can be healed. He often recounted the story of Korah, who rebelled against Moses in the wilderness and perished as the earth opened up and swallowed him and his fellow rebels whole. For Vinnie, this was more than a historical account. He saw each verse as an invitation to examine and cure our own rebellious ways.

Like the city of God, our innermost selves harbor a Holy of Holies from which the River of God emanates. From there, Christ reigns as the Prince of Shalom in whom all harmful things are absent and all beneficial things are present. The river of His Spirit flows through us as streams of insight, grace, and revelation that enable us to listen deeply to the wisdom from above, discern the Spirit's leading, and act accordingly. Just as the eternal city of God is His dwelling place, we are habitations of God through His Spirit (Ephesians 2:22). From the inside out, we are called to live enchanted lives attuned to the currents of the Holy Spirit as they ebb and flow onto the shores of our conscious awareness.

The biggest indicator of healing from our rebellious tendencies is the practice of stillness through which we discover what Jesus is up to and where He is going, so we can go with Him. As we will see in Elijah's life, stillness is essential to the cultivation of deep listening by which we can "behold the works of the LORD" (Psalm 46:8). My prayer is that the Spirit is already awakening in us a fresh hunger and thirst for the kind of knowing we desperately desire in our disenchanted, anxious, and restless world.

Deep Listening and Rest

Listening deeply, we also cultivate the quality of attention that is present when we pray without ceasing. Both practices are forms of active resting that expand our capacity to hear, mature in Christ, and participate in the cross-shaped life (1 Corinthians 2:2; Galatians 2:20). We learn to feed on Him and drink of Him (John 6:53), "embracing a daily death" of self-sacrificial, self-emptying love (1 Corinthians15:31; Philippians 2:5–8).[11]

All of this is inseparable from prophetic consciousness. Remember what John the Revelator heard in one of his many visons on Patmos:

> And the angel said to me, "Write this: Blessed are those who are invited to the marriage supper of the Lamb." And he said to me, "These are true words of God." Then I fell down at his feet to worship him, but he said to me, "You must not do that! I am a fellow servant with you and your comrades who hold the testimony of Jesus. Worship God! For the testimony of Jesus is the spirit of prophecy."

Revelation 19:9–10

This marvelous image captures our relationship with God through the intimate and joyous celebration of the Lamb's wedding supper. Being called to this meal signifies the supreme honor, being

Knowing Where We Come From

chosen by the God of love to witness the kingdom's consummation at a banquet stretching into eternity!

In five decades of serving Christ and helping people, I've seen countless stories of family pain, deep emotional wounds, and scars that persist into adulthood. For many, the idea of a joyous family dinner is unthinkable. Yet this heavenly feast is about experiencing the love that is far beyond all we can ask or think (Ephesians 3:20). This invitation reminds us God desires not only to save us but to maintain close, personal relationship with us. It's about having that special, restful place at the table with Him.

The marriage supper of the Lamb is more than symbolic. It speaks to the heart of our identity as "heirs of God and joint heirs with Christ" (Romans 8:17). This is about our spiritual origins and our part in God's forever family. So take a moment even now to savor your place at God's table. Let the Spirit affirm your value and the deep, abiding union you have with the triune God!

Notice that prior to the passage above from Revelation 19, the judgments against Babylon are pronounced and she is destroyed (Revelation 18). John's vision is a bridge to the Lamb's triumph over all the forces of evil, leading to the endless life of unbroken communion with the Father, Son, and Holy Spirit. When John glimpses the endless feast of love, he is overwhelmed and mistakenly assumes the angelic messenger is Jesus Himself. As John falls down in worship, the angel quickly corrects him, insisting worship should be directed only toward God.

For the record, John mistakenly attempts to worship the angel twice—first in Revelation 19:10 and again in Revelation 22:8–9. Both times the angel rebukes John and redirects his worship. This is in Scripture with good reason. Angel worship was common within the early Christian community, particularly in regions such as Asia Minor, where John oversaw many churches. The angel's correction reinforced the ancient Shema. "Hear, O Israel: The LORD is our God, the LORD alone. You shall love the LORD your God with all your heart, and with all your soul, and with all your might" (Deuteronomy 6:4–5).

John recognized this bedrock of Jewish faith and practice. Even as John the Seer, he realized that what the Shema demanded above a seeing eye was a listening ear. He remembered Moses' words to the Israelites, reminding them of their history with God as they prepared to enter their inheritance. "Then the LORD spoke to you out of the fire. You heard the sound of words but saw no form; there was only a voice" (Deuteronomy 4:12).

The late Rabbi Norman Lamm reminded us why seers need to be accountable:

> Seeing leads to idolatry; the worshiper creates an icon to represent what he saw. Hearing, however, leads to obedience; no physical shape or form beguiles the worshiper. He expresses his devotion in terms of what he has heard, i.e., he obeys the Voice who commands him.[12]

Hearing God is not a onetime event. It demands we cultivate deep listening and wise discerning as a way of life, echoing the angel's declaration that "the testimony of Jesus is the spirit of prophecy" (Revelation 19:10). The testimony of Jesus is the revelation of the Crucified God (the Son) and the Cruciform God (the Father), as made manifest by the Spirit of Prophecy (the Holy Spirit), who reveals and testifies to that which is of Christ (John 16:3; Romans 8:12–17; 1 John 5:5–12). Genuine prophetic messages elevate the Incarnate Son's Person and work and the outworking of both in our lives. As our story becomes integrated with His, His story becomes ours, and the Holy Spirit weaves both together.

Elijah and Listening

As we consider how we might develop the kind of hearing ear God seeks, Elijah's story will meet us where we are in the

Knowing Where We Come From

current culture. The Scriptures portray wide-ranging moments in Elijah's life—not only the dramatic victories and prophetic declarations but also his vulnerabilities, retreats into solitude, and earnest searches for God's voice in the depths of his own dark days. His life is a window into the highs and lows of human experience—not only his but ours.

Elijah's story is about the power of God working through a human being. It also describes a man who is doing his best to serve God while struggling with his own unfinished business. Our study of Elijah goes beyond historical and theological examination; it will invite us into deeper engagement with our own spiritual practices and with our ways of hearing and responding to God. Glimpses into Elijah's life will remind us there can be no effective public witness without a life of private devotion and ongoing communion with God.

Soul-Searching Questions

- Reflect on your current spiritual practices. How will cultivating moments of silence and solitude help you to hear God's voice amid the noise? What specific distractions do you need to eliminate to make this possible?
- In what ways are you currently discerning God's will for your life? How can you incorporate more prayer, Scripture, and spiritual counsel into your discernment process?
- Examine your decision-making process and identify areas in which you might be relying more on your own understanding than on divine guidance. How might Elijah's example help you to address specific fears or uncertainties and make more consistently faith-driven choices?

2

Elijah the Larger-Than-Life Prophet

God has not rejected his people whom he foreknew. Do you not know what the scripture says of Elijah, how he pleads with God against Israel? "Lord, they have killed your prophets, they have demolished your altars; I alone am left, and they are seeking my life."

Romans 11:2–3

In turbulent times, the prophet Elijah resonates as both archetype and beacon. Those in the Pentecostal and Charismatic traditions have long found inspiration in the "spirit of Elijah" (Luke 1:17). This is not only because of his biblical feats but also because of the divine empowerment that defined his spiritual experience, and now defines ours.

Decades ago, during another season of widespread spiritual searching, I heard Bob Mumford speak at a live conference where he articulated the collective yearning for divine presence by asking, "Where is the God of Elijah?" Bob's relentless pursuit of this question produced a profound response. "Where are the Elijahs?" These words underscore the pivotal challenge, not only to seek God's power but to embody the spirit of Elijah today. This need establishes our exploration of Elijah as a model for confronting the complex realities we are facing now.

Elijah's legacy and our struggle are related. As models go, Elijah is a complex figure. His confrontations are dramatic and compelling, but so is his pioneering through a turbulent time in Israel's history. He wrestled with severe conflicts, malign adversaries, inner doubts, and divine mysteries. His trek from survival to transformation required a rugged journey of faith that is meaningful to us, often by way of contrast. The vitriol now evident even on Christian social media platforms departs from the transformative and healing potential Elijah modeled. He never settled for political inroads. Instead, he modeled reform and renewal, challenging the nation and himself to maintain the integrity of their faith. His life invites the modern church to refocus on its core mission rather than being sidetracked by cultural and political entanglements.

Amid the complexities of modern-day pharaohs and princes, culture wars, and political alliances, Elijah's message is critical. Like him, we are called to do more than engage in opposition. We are to undertake transformative actions that align with the kingdom of God—not a top-down kingdom like that of ancient Rome but a bottom-up kingdom where the Crucified God rules and reminds us to live cross-shaped lives.

Elijah's journey was not easy. Even his trip to Mount Horeb, fueled by the desire to encounter God once more, proved painful, shattering his expectations and inviting him into a radically different future. Yet this is part of Elijah's legacy to us. It resonates with our own disappointments and unforeseen struggles, reminding us of his humanity and ours.

Elijah the Larger-Than-Life Prophet

Why We Need Heroes and Heroines

Before we delve into the towering figure of Elijah, we need to understand the human need for heroes and heroines. Our search for such figures starts in childhood. They become personal to us because they help shape our dreams and provide models of resilience, courage, and wisdom. Their stories become part of our narrative identity, the ongoing story we tell ourselves about who we are.[1] This is crucial to how we interpret our lives. It colors our listening (spiritually and otherwise) and contributes to our blind spots. Our narrative identity shapes our existential and spiritual quests.

Cultural icons from my formative years included James Bond, Luke Skywalker, and certain comic book heroes. Throughout my life, social and political figures such as John F. Kennedy, Martin Luther King Jr., Nelson Mandela, and Malala Yousafzai impacted me as they fought for justice and equality. The digital age produced technology icons like Steve Jobs and more recently Elon Musk, innovators whose visionary ways embody the modern archetype of the wizard who uses knowledge and technology to wield influence while sparking disruption and progress, often despite insurmountable odds.

The heroes in my lifetime are too numerous to cover here. Muhammad Ali was a voice for racial pride and resisting war; characters from recent media such as the *Black Panther* films offer a vision of heroism from the long-underrepresented perspective of the African culture and identity. Marvel and DC superheroes have defined and redefined heroism by embodying resilience, justice, and the struggle against evil. Their blend of extraordinary abilities, moral dilemmas, and personal sacrifices resonate with people in all walks of life because their ordeals portray our own struggles on a grand scale.

Heroes and heroines have been elevated throughout human history. Ancient Greece and Rome revered gods, goddesses, demigods, and legendary warriors who showcased supernatural feats and faced complex moral and existential dilemmas. Blending divine attributes with all-too-human conflicts and aspirations, they presaged how we perceive heroism today.

Why are heroic figures so gripping, and why do we identify with them? Psychologically, they offer ways of coping with adversity and overcoming the odds. They embody the traits we aspire to develop. Spiritually, they often stand as beacons of higher moral and ethical standards. They challenge us to live up to our best ideals, and they provide a sense of stability during states of flux. Heroes and heroines help us to anchor our identities and embrace our aspirations.

The Inherent Power of Elijah's Story

Elijah has some things in common with both ancient and modern heroic figures. Like them, he defied what seems possible and elevated our understanding of courage, devotion, and the power of conviction. His radical narrative is marked by extremes, yet his legacy is grounded in what is spiritual and real. He pulls on the thread that runs through humanity's storytelling history, evoking admiration for those who confront the status quo and dare to transcend the ordinary. With its themes of moral conviction and divine power, the Elijah narrative echoes the timeless appeal of heroes who prod us to confront even overwhelming limitations and act with courage and integrity.

Elijah first appears almost superhuman and seems to emerge from out of nowhere. He not only commands the rapt attention of Ahab and Jezebel but rivets our attention with a presence so formidable it seems to leap off the pages. Within both the Jewish and the Christian traditions, Elijah transcends mere reverence. He becomes a paragon of unyielding zeal, a quintessential prophet of fire, whose boldness knows no bounds. He embodies a spirit that confronts but also consumes, leaving no room for compromise.

The beginning of the Elijah narrative sweeps us up in its urgency, intrigue, mystery, and movement. His sudden appearance in the scriptural record and his dramatic actions captivate our imaginations while challenging us to probe the myriad spiritual undercurrents running through his experience. He is an archetypal figure, "an ideal, prototype or symbol that represents something core or foundational in human experience."[2]

Archetypes are like blueprints that outline the traits and themes we all recognize. Archetypal figures help us to understand ourselves and the roles we play. They reflect patterns of behavior and deep truths that are ingrained in the human spirit. In this regard, Elijah embodies qualities that touch us on an instinctual level. As we follow Jesus, we might not deliberately or consciously engage with Elijah's story as a prayerful exercise, but Elijah's qualities and actions resonate with our deeper spiritual inclinations, much the way the Spirit groans within us "with groanings too deep for words" (Romans 8:26 NASB).

I believe this connection usually happens subtly. As a prophetic archetype, Elijah reflects our inherent understanding of courage, faith, and justice as themes embedded within our Christian tradition. When we read about how he stood alone against the prophets of Baal, it strikes a chord within us and stirs responses that align with the archetypal patterns. It is more than learning a moral lesson; it's about sensing an underlying internal resonance that encourages us to emulate the portrayed qualities in our own lives.

This happens because the scriptural Elijah narrative is hidden in a chamber room of the heart, below the level of our immediate awareness. Yet when the strength of that story is needed, the Spirit stirs up the instinct and perhaps even the way we imagine Elijah, and we find ourselves energized by a memory stored for such a time as this. It is important we listen to it, act on it, and take courage when needed.

In a relativist world of daunting challenges, Elijah remains a symbol of unwavering conviction and divine fervor. His life testifies to the power of faith and action. His dramatic confrontations and deep devotion speak to our need for figures who not only embody but also enact their beliefs in transformative ways.

Therefore, we will approach Elijah as more than a prophet of ancient times; he is a mirror reflecting our modern spiritual and existential dilemmas. This backdrop is crucial as we explore the ways in which Elijah's life can provoke us to listen more deeply and act more courageously.

Reconnected through Story

Our interactions with stories like Elijah's spark our ability to listen to God's direction. In his classic work, *The Prophetic Imagination*, Walter Brueggemann explains that our consumer-driven culture is "organized against history."[3] We have been caught up in the culture and have abandoned the faith tradition,[4] resulting in a "depreciation of memory and a ridicule of hope" that disconnects us from the past and strips away all but what is happening now.[5]

This is the fruit of postmodernity—and we wonder why so many among us are battling depression! We naively denigrate the past, not realizing that doing so devalues the future. When both lose their worth, the present also suffers, leading directly to despair, depression, and disconnection from any potentially energizing historical anchor. The final step in the process is the devaluing of self.

Remember that without a prophetic vision, we risk disintegration (Proverbs 29:18). Walter Brueggemann emphasizes the role of prophetic imagination in providing us with "energizing memories and radical hopes."[6] Authentic prophetic vision is embedded in the energizing memories of our covenant history with God. This vision wards off disintegration. Consider the stories that form the backbone of our faith: Abraham and Sarah, the forebears of our faith; Jacob, who dreamt of the ladder reaching to heaven and wrestled with the angel; Joseph, whose dreams sustained him through thirteen years of tribulation until they were realized; Moses, who encountered God at the burning bush and led the Israelites across the Red Sea. These aren't just stories! They are sacred, inspired, and prophetic words from God. When we hold them in our hearts, they become sources of strength that shape our spiritual instincts and help us to recognize divine guidance. Engaging in deep, instinctual listening can guide us toward actions that are true to our faith and resonate with the divine justice and mercy Elijah championed.

Engaging with figures such as Elijah reconnects the past and present, enriches our interior experience, and enhances our spiritual perception and responsiveness. As archetype, Elijah becomes a focal point around which we gather and derive inspiration. Whenever we speak of "the spirit of Elijah," we sense an undeniable energy and animation coming alive among us. We share a collective admiration as we remember his confrontations with false prophets and kings, his boldness and fidelity, his calling down of fire from heaven, and his dramatic affecting of the natural elements.

Like Moses, the original paradigm prophet (Deuteronomy 33:1), Elijah is the "man of God," a voice of truth and moral courage in a world of widespread deceit and moral decline (2 Kings 1:12). His impact extends beyond his physical presence, and his legacy is so potent he is thought to return at pivotal times, as prophesied in Malachi 4:5–6, to turn the hearts of the younger generation back to their elders, and as such to God, before the "great and terrible day of the LORD comes." This expectation cements Elijah as a historical figure and a symbol of the people's messianic hopes. It is no wonder his memory energizes our collective memory!

Elijah Speaks to Us, Now

Elijah's story speaks to themes of justice, spiritual power, and moral integrity in every generation. As inheritors of these narratives, we are challenged by Elijah's archetype to respond to societal and spiritual decay. His life prompts us to consider our roles in confronting modern-day idols and injustices, with truth and righteousness. Thus, Elijah transcends his own story. We hear his voice in our imaginations, enlivened by the breath of God's Spirit. His larger-than-life presence invites us to engage with our world and hold fast our convictions, knowing our actions are being woven into the larger divine narrative.

While we are inspired and elated by this idea, we need to remember that the archetype does not exclude or discard Elijah's moments of vulnerability and personal struggle. His experiences of fear, exhaustion, and even despair are equally a part of the archetype. These signs of his humanity remind us that our spiritual journeys are not only about our moments of power and triumph. They are also about facing our wilderness seasons, seeking divine sustenance during our famines, and listening for the still, small voice amid the storms. By embracing both the strengths and vulnerabilities of Elijah, we can approach our faith with a more balanced and compassionate perspective, striving not only for the "fireworks" but also valuing the quiet, introspective times that shape our spiritual maturity.

The fireworks will come after Elijah confronts Ahab and declares, "As the LORD the God of Israel lives, before whom I stand, there shall be neither dew nor rain these years, except by my word" (1 Kings 17:1). His bold proclamation does not occur in a vacuum. To stand in the courts of Ahab is to stand before a deeply compromised Omride king and a Phoenician

Elijah the Larger-Than-Life Prophet

queen whose allegiance to Baal is evidenced by 850 prophets of Baal and Ashtaroth. Elijah's audacious claim of controlling the weather on God's behalf is an affront to Ahab and Jezebel's conviction that Baal is the source of all rain. What the king and queen fail to realize in that heated moment is Elijah is determined to have a showdown with Baal. He is throwing down the gauntlet in order to expose Baal as a fraud. The people will realize Baal cannot provide rain when they desperately need it. This provocation and Baal's ensuing humiliation are so profound we can only ask, "Who is this man who abruptly appears in the scriptural narrative, and what compels him to confront such formidable adversaries?"

We are about to find out!

Soul-Searching Questions

- What are the qualities or actions of heroes and heroines that most resonate with you or challenge you? How do these qualities or actions shed light on your narrative identity? What potential areas of growth do they bring to mind?
- Which heroes or heroines have most profoundly impacted your values, sense of self, aspirations, personal development, and spiritual growth? Which of the qualities or actions they embody expose blind spots in your own life?
- In your spiritual journey, who has served as a heroic figure by inspiring you to deepen your faith, cultivate resilience, or pursue a life of purpose and meaning? How has this figure affected your ability to perceive God's voice and discern His will for your life?

3

Journeying with Elijah: The Tishbite and His Call

Now Elijah the Tishbite, who was of the settlers of Gilead, said to Ahab, "As the LORD, the God of Israel lives, before whom I stand, surely there shall be neither dew nor rain these years, except by my word."

1 Kings 17:1 NASB

As we approach the heart of Elijah's story, we see his struggles, triumphs, and divine calling unfold. But our first glimpse of him in 1 Kings 17:1 offers no grand announcement or elaborate introduction. Elijah simply steps onto the scene and delivers God's stark message to King Ahab. *A drought is coming.* Unlike other prophets, who are introduced with "The word of the Lord came to so and so," Elijah simply bursts forth and blurts out what he came to say. He is as a man driven by an inner, divine impulse—a man who embodies the very power of the Spirit.

Elijah's origins are mysterious. He's called "the Tishbite," and scholars believe this points to a small, almost forgotten town called Tishbe in Upper Galilee. Tishbe's exact location is uncertain. Some scholars suggest it is not a place but a group or social class. Elijah was possibly a displaced person, perhaps a settler driven there by conflicts or invasions. In any case, God called Elijah, a man from an unassuming place, into a momentous calling.

We do know Elijah settled in Gilead, which lay east of the Jordan, between the Yarmuk River to the north and an indistinct southern boundary near the Dead Sea. The Jabbok River (the modern Zarqa River) bisected Gilead, making the land lush and fertile. The tribe of Manasseh gradually settled the dense forests in the region's northern half. The tribe of Gad occupied the central lands around the Jabbok, and the Reubenites held the southern territory.

Scripture does not detail the region's history in Elijah's day, but as a settler and a prophet, he would have been impacted by the ongoing struggle to control this rich, strategic region. Depending upon Elijah's own tribal affiliation (or lack thereof), Gilead's division among three Israelite tribes would also impact him. Although the tribes were united under the banner of Israel, territorial or leadership disputes could erupt at any time.[1] Whether Elijah chose to settle in a politically unstable region or felt he had no other options, he called Gilead home.

Long before Elijah's time, Israel's patriarchs and prophets walked Gilead's rugged paths and encountered God. Gilead became a place of divine revelation and significant covenantal history, with Jacob's divine encounters being part of this legacy. In this area, Jacob wrestled with the angel and solidified his place in Israel's story (Genesis 32:24–30). Gilead was also the place from which Jephthah, a judge of Israel, hailed (Judges 11:1–11). As was true of Jacob, Jephthah's story of redemption and leadership became an important part of Israel's collective memory.

Journeying with Elijah: The Tishbite and His Call

It may be that these historical and spiritual associations influenced Elijah's choice to settle in Gilead. For a prophet called to confront the idolatry and spiritual waywardness of Israel, living there could have easily evoked the sense of divine presence and purpose that marked his predecessors' lives. As Elijah wrestled with his call, Gilead's history of covenant faithfulness may have strengthened and affirmed his sense of God's enduring promises and transformative power. This sense of the place seems perfectly aligned with Elijah's mission to call Israel back to faithfulness.

Such resonances would feed Elijah's deep sense of connection to his people's covenant history and remind him of the long line of faithful servants who had preceded him in God's service. As he navigated the turbulence of his times, such links to the past could only have helped Elijah to stand firm in an uncertain present.

Standing Firm and Being Spiritually Formed

Against the backdrop of shifting political allegiances and other external tensions, Elijah had to learn to stand firm. As a solitary but intense figure walking Gilead's paths, his heart must have burned with passion for Yahweh and His people, the local Baal worship tearing at his soul. For a man so devoted to Yahweh, the relentless assault on the sacred covenant would have been a source of perpetual grief.

In the quiet moments when dark shadows of demonic deception danced around Elijah's fellow Israelites, an agony of questions would have gnawed at his spirit. How could his people forsake the God who had led them through the wilderness, parted the seas, and rained down manna from heaven? What drove them to bow before lifeless idols and abandon the path of righteousness? How could they succumb to the fleeting pleasures of false gods?

Like Elijah, we face struggles, hardships, hard questions, and the need to exchange the familiar for the unfamiliar. Elijah's life mirrors God's call to His people to trust and obey, even when the path is uncertain, as it was for Abraham and his successors. We are all on a journey of spiritual formation, being shaped and molded by God's Spirit. This spiritual journey is not only about learning more or doing more; it is a matter of becoming more like Christ in our inner lives. It's about deepening our relationship with God, often through the trials and challenges we face. Like Elijah, we are learning to trust God completely, rely on His guidance, and stand firm in our calling, no matter the odds. This is the stuff of spiritual formation, God's ongoing work in shaping our character, attitudes, and actions. Our spiritual formation includes practices such as prayer, Scripture meditation, and obedience to God's leading. All of it transforms us and helps us to grow in our capacity to love God and others, so that in our moments of faith and challenge, we draw closer to God and fulfill our divine purpose.

This is part of God's unfolding intent for *your* life. Embrace it, trusting that through every challenge, you are being formed and shaped by God's own hand to become who you are meant to be in Christ, through His Spirit.

Prophetic Legitimacy and the Divine Council

In the realm of prophetic ministry, legitimacy is paramount. From the first mention of Elijah in Scripture, he is identified as a prophet. All prophets faced difficulty and opposition, and all of them made predictions. But were these the marks of a true prophet under the Mosaic economy? Were accurate predictions the main indicator of a prophet's authenticity? We know Balaam delivered four accurate prophecies. Yet he was a false prophet (Numbers 23:9–10, 21–24; 24:5–9, 17). Elijah, a God-appointed prophet, accurately declared before Ahab, Jezebel,

Journeying with Elijah: The Tishbite and His Call

and 850 false prophets that he would control the rain. It took three and a half years, but his prophecy proved valid.

True prophets foretell events to come, but the prophetic isn't merely about the foretelling of events or demonstration of supernatural power. True prophetic legitimacy stems from a deeper, more profound connection with the divine. Jeremiah 23:18 captures this essential connection perfectly, asking, "For who has stood in the council of the LORD so as to see and to hear his word? Who has given heed to his word so as to proclaim it?" This passage highlights the critical difference between true prophets and false ones—the former stand in the divine council, seeing and hearing the word of Yahweh. The latter do not.

Elijah and the Council

When we consider Elijah, we see legitimacy anchored in this divine reality. Although there is no scriptural record of how he might have been initiated into the divine council, his declaration before King Ahab offers insight. Standing in the wicked king's court and in the presence of his queen, Jezebel, and the court prophets of Baal and Asherah, Elijah asserted he stood in the presence of Yahweh. This is not a rhetorical statement but a veiled reference to his place in the heavenly council. To Ahab and those around him, Elijah may have appeared as a lone, eccentric man, yet Elijah knew that God, His throne, and all the attendants surrounding His throne backed his proclamation.

Elijah's confidence in this invisible reality were further illustrated in his final moments on earth. As he prepared to depart by whirlwind, his soon-to-be successor, Elisha, asked for a double portion of Elijah's spirit. Elijah's response was telling. He said, "You have asked a hard thing. Nevertheless, if you see me when I am taken from you, it shall be so for you; but if not, it shall not be so" (2 Kings 2:10 LSB). The emphasis is not on seeing Elijah, but on perceiving the divine chariot and the heavenly hosts—a moment that signified the tearing open of the veil between the earthly and the heavenly. Thus, Elisha was inducted into the heavenly council, to see and hear the word of Yahweh.

Council Prophets Counter False Prophets and Magical Thinking

Being inducted into the heavenly council legitimizes a prophet's claim as a true messenger of God. Foresight and predictions are insufficient in verifying a prophet's authenticity. The role of a prophet encompasses a broader spectrum of divine insights and guidance, and entrance into the heavenly council is requisite. The prophet Jeremiah made the ultimate criteria plain:

> Thus says the LORD of hosts: Do not listen to the words of the prophets who prophesy to you; they are deluding you. They speak visions of their own minds, not from the mouth of the LORD. They keep saying to those who despise the word of the LORD, "It shall be well with you"; and to all who stubbornly follow their own stubborn hearts, they say, "No calamity shall come upon you."
>
> *For who has stood in the council of the LORD so as to see and to hear his word?* Who has given heed to his word so as to proclaim it?
>
> Jeremiah 23:16–18, emphasis added

When Jeremiah uttered these words, he alone declared the dangers and duplicity of false prophets, including those who assured King Zedekiah of peace where there was no peace. Their lies comforted the king but deluded him. The king favored the court prophets who not only misled him but also actively opposed Jeremiah—even having him thrown into a pit in the palace and branding *him* as the false prophet.

Jeremiah upheld the true prophetic legitimacy that is rooted in the divine encounter of standing in the council of the Lord, seeing and hearing His word and faithfully proclaiming it to His people. It is apparent the source informing Jeremiah's prophetic words was not the source on which Zedekiah's court prophets relied. Jeremiah was the lone voice of truth in a chorus of deceit. In much the way Elijah challenged Ahaziah's confidence in Baal's prophets, Jeremiah cautioned the king not to trust those who bore false witness. Jeremiah was not afraid to oppose imposters. At great risk to himself, he said what he knew was true, that all of Judah would be divinely judged and taken captive to Babylon for seventy years.

The contrast Jeremiah drew between true prophecy and false promises marked a critical moment in Judah's history. The dark clouds of exile were already rolling in, yet the court prophets continued spouting falsehoods. Even while Babylon's armies laid siege to Jerusalem, the court prophets predicted peace. Their magical thinking embraced unrealistic expectations and beliefs not based in reality. It thrived on the people's desire for comfort and was fed by cognitive biases that deluded them into believing their thoughts alone could influence the world, and that the fact of their thoughts being formed was a sign that they reflected reality.[2] So they blatantly ignored God's warnings and persisted in their rebellion.

When God speaks, He does not indulge our desires for comfort through magical thinking. Instead, He often challenges us, as when He made Samuel's ears tingle with a hard truth about the impending judgment on Eli's house (1 Samuel 3:11–14). When God's people find themselves in compromising situations, God's words aim to awaken and recalibrate their cognition, not reinforce their complacency.

Understanding the Council of the Lord

The truth of standing in God's council has often been ignored and misinterpreted. Yet from Moses to Malachi, God's council was the qualifying factor for true prophetic ministry.

Council and *counsel* are very different words. *Counsel* refers to advice or guidance and is often used regarding the work that lawyers do. *Council* refers to an assembly of people who meet to make decisions. In a governmental or organizational context, a council typically involves deliberation and decision-making among the members.

The word *council* is crucial to our discussion. It implies not just hearing God's word as advice but standing in His presence, being part of the deliberative process by which God's will is revealed and decisions are made. Jeremiah 23:18 highlights the exclusive privilege of truly knowing and understanding God's will. This is what separates true prophets from the false ones who claim to speak for God. Imposters are not part of God's council. They claim to have divine insight without having the authentic, profound experience of God's revelatory presence.

Confusing *council* with *counsel* means missing the depth of the relationship and authority the true prophetic implies and reduces it to the receiving of advice. Similarly, *the council of the Lord* is not just any meeting place in which deliberations on the affairs of both heaven and earth take place. It is depicted as a dynamic gathering of divinely appointed angelic agents and humans who are divinely chosen to participate. God Himself presides over this divine assembly vividly portrayed in the creation narrative in Genesis, the heavenly visions seen by Isaiah in the temple, and the divine councils discussed in 1 Kings and Ezekiel.

The council highlights God's relational nature. The gathering isn't only about His commands. True prophets like Elijah actually *stood* in the council, not as passive recipients of God's plans but as active participants in divine conversations. Isaiah stood there by ecstatic vision (Isaiah 6:1–13). Moses participated from the foot of Mount Horeb (also known as Mount Sinai) in Exodus 3 and from the top of Mount Sinai in Exodus

19:3–6. Ezekiel's experience in the council occurred at the river Chebar (Ezekiel 1:26–28).

These interactions accentuate God's very personal, self-revealing interaction with His creation, and particularly His prophets in the Mosaic economy. This personal interface with God involved much more than transmitting information; it transformed the prophet, who then embodied God's word and brought the divine will into the earthly arena. This transformative aspect of ancient prophecy distinguished true prophets from false ones, as true prophets conveyed not only foresight but the heart and judgment of God in order to align the people's hearts with His will.

In Jeremiah 23:16–18, the Lord called to account the prophets who spoke of peace where no peace existed. They were not authentic prophets. They had not experienced the divine council or encountered the Preexistent Christ (the Word of Yahweh in John 1:1 and the "Angel of Yahweh" in Exodus 3:2). God's ancient prophets had ongoing encounters with the One later known as Jesus. Skeptics might question how Old Testament figures could have seen Him before His birth in Bethlehem. However, in the mystery of God's eternal nature, Jesus said, "Before Abraham was, I am" (John 8:58).

The Council Today

Under the Mosaic economy, standing in the divine council was a privilege that allowed prophets to see and hear the Lord directly, ensuring the divine inspiration of their communications. The advent of New Testament realities expanded the landscape of divine communication through the Person and Work of the Incarnate Son, and the outpouring of the Holy Spirit. This shift democratized the experience of divine communication, making it accessible to all believers, not just a select few. Scholars such as Roger Stronstad articulate this concept as the "prophethood of all believers,"[3] suggesting that although not all are called to be prophets in the formal sense Ephesians 4 describes, every believer has the capacity to hear and discern the will of God.

The apostle Paul said every follower of Christ has been called into "the fellowship of [God's] Son" (1 Corinthians 1:9 NKJV). By the indwelling Spirit, we participate with the Son in the endless communion that is the love of God the Father. Communing with the triune God from the inside out empowers us to live in a type of continual divine council, where we can receive guidance, wisdom, and insight directly from the Spirit. This transformative process reflects our communal and personal responsibility to discern God's voice and actively participate in faith in the testimony of Jesus, the Spirit of Prophecy Himself (Revelation 19:10).

If we can embrace this broader understanding of prophetic function, we can discover what T. Austin Sparks said many decades ago. "The prophetic function, going far beyond mere events, happenings and dates, is the ministry of spiritual interpretation. That phrase will cover the whole ground of that with which we are now concerned. Prophecy is spiritual interpretation."[4]

Sparks speaks of interpreting everything from a spiritual perspective, thereby unveiling the spiritual implications of past, present, and future events, and presenting them to the people of God. The essence of prophetic function and expression is in understanding the spiritual meaning and significance behind the events we perceive.

Elijah's Decree: The Withholding of Rain and Dew

At the very outset of his first task, Elijah had to delineate the cause of a coming catastrophic event. So he told Ahab, "As the LORD the God of Israel lives, before whom I stand, there shall be neither dew nor rain these years, except by my word"

Journeying with Elijah: The Tishbite and His Call

(1 Kings 17:1). Elijah's appearance seemed sudden, but his message was not out of the blue; it was straight from the following Torah text:[5]

> "It shall be that if you earnestly obey My commandments which I command you today, to love the LORD your God and serve Him with all your heart and with all your soul, then I will give you the rain for your land in its season, the early rain and the latter rain, that you may gather in your grain, your new wine, and your oil. And I will send grass in your fields for your livestock, that you may eat and be filled." Take heed to yourselves, lest your heart be deceived, and you turn aside and serve other gods and worship them, lest the LORD's anger be aroused against you, and He shut up the heavens so that there be no rain, and the land yield no produce, and you perish quickly from the good land which the LORD is giving you.
>
> Deuteronomy 11:13–17 NKJV

I highly doubt Elijah had a priestly copy of the Torah. Yet as a faithful Hebrew, he knew what it said. James adds a piece of the story, writing,

> The effective, fervent prayer of a righteous man avails much. Elijah was a man with a nature like ours, and *he prayed earnestly that it would not rain; and it did not rain on the land for three years and six months.* And he prayed again, and the heaven gave rain, and the earth produced its fruit.
>
> James 5:16–18 NKJV, emphasis added

Notice the portion of text I italicized. James is telling us that prior to this critical moment in King Ahab's court, Elijah had already "shut up" the heavens by effectual, fervent prayer (Luke 4:25). James' assertion is intriguing, especially because the Old Testament doesn't specifically mention the event prior to 1 Kings 17.

Prophetic Integrity and the Elijah Legacy

There are, however, factors to consider about James' statement.

- Although the Old Testament does not explicitly record Elijah's prayer to shut up the heavens prior to 1 Kings 17, it is possible such an event was part of the oral tradition that preserved and transmitted stories and teachings within Jewish communities throughout Israelite history.[6]
- James, as a Jewish leader writing to a Jewish audience, may have drawn upon the oral tradition that was widely known and accepted among his audience.
- The oral tradition encompassed a "range of methods for the spoken transmission and preservation in memory of non-written verbal information; or a particular case of information so transmitted."[7]
- The reference to Elijah's letter to Jehoram in 2 Chronicles 21 raises interesting questions about the full extent of Elijah's ministry and how it is recorded in the biblical narrative. While we might speculate that not all of Elijah's works are captured in the canonical record, we cannot make this assertion with certainty based solely on the biblical text. The Canon does not explicitly state that all of Elijah's deeds were recorded, although it is plausible. When considering James' reference to Elijah's prayer in James 5:17–18, it is possible James was drawing from oral tradition or simply deducing this based on the teachings in Deuteronomy (such as 11:16–17) regarding the cessation of rain as a consequence of the people forgetting God. While this might be a reasoned deduction from Scripture, we cannot ignore the possibility that James was writing under the inspiration of the Holy Spirit and was granted insight into Elijah's life not explicitly recorded in the Old Testament. The

Bible does not directly state that all of Elijah's deeds were unrecorded, but it does leave room for divine revelation beyond the recorded narrative. Elijah's role as a prophet, performing miracles and demonstrating great faith, was well known within the Jewish tradition, and James' reference could reflect a broader understanding of his ministry. Nonetheless, the integrity of James' statement remains intact, as it reflects a faithful interpretation rooted in the wider theological context of Elijah's prophetic witness and God's covenant relationship with Israel.

- James may also have drawn upon this broader understanding of Elijah's character to make his point about the effectiveness of prayer.

- James' statement might also carry a deeper spiritual meaning than a strictly literal one. He could be using Elijah as an example of the power of prayer and the effectiveness of the prayers of righteous individuals, rather than providing a historical account of specific events in Elijah's life.

My personal sense is James was somehow privy to the fact that prior to his public appearance, Elijah had established a place of intercession in regard to rain. Thus, he had already obtained the witness from the Lord that there would be no rain until he (Elijah) delivered the word of reversal that Yahweh entrusted to him.

Speech-Act Theory

Apart from speech that is divinely inspired, genuine history-making, life-altering words are not spoken. Such words are sacred "speech-acts" described in "speech-act theory,"[8] which involves the three aspects of speech described below in relation to the Elijah narrative:

- The locutionary act releases a "meaningful utterance."[9] Elijah speaks the words, stating there will be no rain except by his word. His statement is clear and has a specific meaning.
- The illocutionary act involves a more specific, "assertive" statement, a kind of "performance" of the message.[10] This is where the power lies. Elijah isn't making a weather forecast; he's delivering a divine decree. Because he is speaking on God's behalf, his words carry the weight of divine authority. His prophetic pronouncement is therefore an act of divine intervention in the natural order.
- The perlocutionary act "seeks to change behavior."[11] The drought that follows is not coincidental; it directly results from Elijah's prophetic declaration. His words effect a significant change, both in the land and in the people's hearts.

Now consider the following scene in relation to speech-act theory. Elijah, the prophet of God, stands before King Ahab and declares, "As the LORD the God of Israel lives, before whom I stand, there shall be neither dew nor rain these years, except by my word" (1 Kings 17:1). This encounter with Ahab demonstrates language that accomplishes more than communication; it becomes a vehicle for divine action. Elijah's words shaped history in accordance with God's will. Mind you, only the experiential knowing of the Spirit could empower Elijah to call something that was not as though it was (Romans 4:17). He had already cultivated a maturity where listening and discernment were concerned, and it did not happen overnight. He had prayed long and hard and in a sustained manner, for how

Journeying with Elijah: The Tishbite and His Call

long we do not know. This happened *before* 1 Kings 17:1, and it birthed in him the confidence to come out of hiding, stand in the king's court, and make his bold assertion.

While James' mention of Elijah's prayer raises questions about the Old Testament's omission of this detail, the broader context of oral tradition, inspired interpretation, contextual understanding, and spiritual insight help us to find resolution. James likely aimed to stress the significance and effectiveness of fervent, persistent prayer. The idea is that we do not always come to understanding in an instant. Consider Moses' encounter with God at the burning bush. God instructed him to throw down his rod, and it immediately transformed into a snake. Then God told him to pick up the rod again (Exodus 4:1–5).

We perhaps take much for granted when we read this passage. Do we honestly believe that a single attempt at throwing down and picking up the rod convinced Moses of the outcome God described? Knowing human nature, that is not likely! We as human beings must learn new things and practice certain tasks until we're confident they will yield the desired results. Being human means grappling with doubts and fears—even for those who have practiced in the presence of the Angel of Yahweh!

We can't know how long Elijah prayed and interceded until he felt confident enough to publicly declare his commission to shut off the rain and eventually restore it. Stories like his remind us that faith and conviction rarely manifest as instantaneous certainties. Most often, they grow through persistent practice and prayer. I say this in hopes of dispelling the myth that we get "downloads" from God. Machines get downloads, and we are not machines.

You are not a machine but a human being who has to slow down to the speed of life for an honest, self-aware, and God-aware person. That means accepting that God made you to be human. It means realizing that, like me and everybody since

Adam, you are in some ways a mess, and as hard as you try to do good, everything you do is touched by your flaws and weaknesses.

This is our reality as human beings. It takes faith and patience to inherit the promises of God (Hebrews 6:12). The call to maturity is not a download. It is a gradual walk through the training of your spiritual senses to discern good and evil. That takes time—lots and lots of time.

Consider Elijah. He "was a man with a nature like ours, and he prayed earnestly that it would not rain; and it did not rain on the land for three years and six months" (James 5:17 NKJV). There were times in his hiding and obscurity when he had to "pray through," as the saints of former generations describe it. He had to pray through his doubts, fears, anxieties, uncertainties, and the negative slant he had developed through whatever hardships he endured before settling in Gilead. He had to learn how to cling to the flickering flame of faith within him. He learned to utter prayers of intercession for himself and his wayward brethren. He practiced beseeching Yahweh to turn their hearts back to him.

Gilead, where Elijah settled, was no Garden of Eden. It was a land of turmoil and discontentment. Elijah found himself drawn into its chaos as a reluctant witness to simmering tensions that threatened to boil over. Amid the shifting alliances of rival factions, Elijah learned to stand as a beacon of hope. Yet all the while, his internal struggles mirrored the unrest surrounding him. His history, as captured in the scriptural narrative, reveals he wrestled with doubts, fears, and the weight of his own inadequacies. Still, he clung to the promise of Yahweh's faithfulness, trusting that even in his darkest hour, the light of divine providence would guide him.

As he declared his God-appointed authority over the weather, Elijah did not know all that lay ahead. But keep reading! Our journey with the Tishbite continues as some of his greatest, most difficult, and most telling experiences unfold.

Journeying with Elijah: The Tishbite and His Call

Soul-Searching Questions

- How do you maintain faith and hope during periods of uncertainty and turmoil? Reflecting on your times of wrestling with doubts and inadequacies, how might you cultivate a posture of trust and reliance on God's faithfulness as Elijah did?

- Describe your practice of "praying through" your doubts, fears, and anxieties when circumstances seem overwhelming. What specific strategies help you cling to the flame of faith when it seems to flicker within you?

- Which Scriptures, prayers, or spiritual practices can you draw upon to anchor your soul, restore your hope, and remind you of God's unwavering presence with you?

4

Look What the Wind Blew In (to Ahab's Court)

> Elijah was a human being like us, and he prayed fervently that it might not rain, and for three years and six months it did not rain on the earth. Then he prayed again, and the heaven gave rain and the earth yielded its harvest.
>
> James 5:17–18

Elijah wasn't a man who adapted himself to the culture or to the expectations of those in power. He committed himself not to facts on the ground but to the will and word of God. As a prophet living in a corrupted land, this devotion made him a thorn in the side of Ahab, Jezebel, and anyone who toed their line. Elijah's person and ministry were formed by prayer, communion, and his solitary reflections in Gilead. These contributed to his courage in proclaiming before Ahab that there would be neither dew nor rain except by his decree. Elijah certainly needed that kind of courage to declare such things to a king in Ahab's pressurized and powerful position.

For Ahab, Elijah was, at best, an annoyance. The king failed to realize that God had authorized Elijah not only to prophesy drought but to enforce its duration. As noted in the previous chapter, Elijah was not offering a weather forecast; he was delivering a Spirit-inspired utterance of power that would shake the nation's foundations, destabilize Ahab's sense of control, and solidify Elijah's role in Israel's imagination and history.

It's crucial to note that Elijah's warning extended beyond the absence of rain to include the absence even of dew, resulting in hopelessly parched land. To this day, drought occurs in that region when the usual dry season persists past its "natural cycle of April through September."[1] Extended dry seasons are troublesome; yet they do not obliterate the formation of dew essential to trees and crops. The suspension of dew that Elijah announced would be an extraordinary event and nothing less than a national catastrophe.[2]

Downward Spiral and a Prophetic Signal

The question is how the people of God found themselves in such a dire situation. Solomon offers insight, writing, "When a land rebels it has many rulers; but with an intelligent ruler there is lasting order" (Proverbs 28:2). By the time Ahab (the Northern Kingdom's seventh king) came to the throne, Israel had been in a deep spiral for generations. Beginning with the wicked reign of Jeroboam and continuing through the dynasty of Omri and his son Ahab, each ruler seemed more corrupt than his predecessor.

This pattern ultimately led to the kingdom's downfall. Assyria's king, Tiglath Pileser III, eventually destroyed the Northern Kingdom, and Assyria scattered God's people across its empire. Ahab was one evil king of many, but Scripture is clear about the role of his rulership, stating, "Ahab son of Omri did evil in the sight of the LORD more than all who were before him" (1 Kings 16:30). Clearly, Ahab's behavior was a serious departure from Israel's religious teachings. "And as if it had been a light thing for him to walk in the sins of Jeroboam son of Nebat, he took as his wife Jezebel daughter of King Ethbaal of the Sidonians, and went and served Baal, and worshiped him" (1 Kings 16:31).

Ahab's promotion of Baal worship led to the compromise that brought Elijah out of hiding. First Kings 16:32–33 says of Ahab, "He erected an altar for Baal in the house of Baal, which he built in Samaria. Ahab also made a sacred pole. Ahab did more to provoke the anger of the LORD, the God of Israel, than had all the kings of Israel who were before him."

Elijah's sudden appearance in King Ahab's court was not a social call or business meeting. The Spirit carried the prophet there, and Elijah stood boldly before the throne and the false prophets. He did not adhere to the court's royal protocols but was known for his forthright and commanding presence, as described in the books of 1 and 2 Kings. He more than likely bypassed the formalities. This breach of protocol was a powerful, divinely sanctioned signal of an imminent spiritual showdown.

Elijah and Aslan

If you are a C. S. Lewis fan, you are probably familiar with a certain conversation from *The Lion, the Witch and the Wardrobe* when the Pevensie children (Peter, Susan, Edmund, and Lucy) ask Mr. Beaver about Aslan the King (who is a Christ figure). Here is what Mr. Beaver says in a poem about Aslan:

> Wrong will be right, when Aslan comes in sight,
> At the sound of his roar, sorrows will be no more,
> When he bares his teeth, winter meets its death,
> And when he shakes his mane, we shall have spring again.

Susan wants to see this Aslan. Mr. Beaver assures her he brought her and her siblings to the woods with that in mind. He also reveals that Aslan is not a man, as she supposes, but a lion—in fact, Aslan is the King, and the son of the great "Emperor-beyond-the-Sea."

Taken aback, Susan wants to know whether Aslan is "safe." "Safe?" asks Mr. Beaver. "Don't you hear what Mrs. Beaver tells you? Who said anything about safe? 'Course he isn't safe. But he's good. He's the King, I tell you."

Nor is Aslan tame. As Mr. Beaver warns,

> He'll be coming and going. . . . One day you'll see him and another you won't. He doesn't like being tied down—and of course he has other countries to attend to. It's quite all right. He'll often drop in. Only you mustn't press him. He's wild, you know. Not like a tame lion.[3]

Elijah is not the Christ figure that Aslan is. But Elijah shares some of Aslan's traits and is linked with Christ in Scripture, as Mark's and Luke's gospels make clear. Like Aslan, Elijah is neither benign nor easily understood. He presents not as tame but as wild, not as safe but as good. In his prophetic role, Elijah is fiercely loyal to God and his calling, often putting him at odds with the royal authority and societal norms. Unlike the court prophets of Ahab and Jezebel, Elijah is not expedient and will not prophesy that which is socially expected or politically correct.

Just as Aslan moves in mysterious ways, appearing and disappearing in Narnia according to a greater plan known only to him, Elijah's movements and actions are dictated by his communion with God. Both figures, though seemingly dangerous and unpredictable, operate under a moral framework that is inherently good and just—they are driven by the singular divine purpose that transcends human understanding.

Elijah and Jesus

Elijah's prophetic role starkly contrasts with that of typical court prophets in his day who often aligned their messages with the political and religious agendas of the royal court and favored the reigning king's interests. Unlike them, Elijah stood firm in delivering God's true words, regardless of their unpopularity or potential risk to him as the messenger. This independence from royal influence highlights the integrity that made Elijah's prophetic mission so personally challenging yet crucial to Israel's spiritual health.

Elijah's resistance to pressure from the ruling powers foreshadows Jesus in His role as Prophet. Jesus steadfastly refused to conform to His contemporaries' expectations. Throughout His ministry, Jesus challenged prevailing interpretations of the law and the prophets, often clashing with Judaism's powerful religious leaders. Jesus' teachings often overturned conventional views, emphasizing the spirit of the law rather than the letter and advocating a deeper, more personal relationship with God that transcends traditional boundaries and practices.

Jesus' approach to prophecy did not cater to popular expectations or opinions. Political expediency and the agendas of ruling powers had no place with Him. Instead, He addressed the deeper issues that placed Him in direct conflict with the Pharisees and Sadducees who feared losing the power and control they had amassed. His parables and sermons, like the Sermon on the Mount, pushed against legalistic interpretations of religious law and urged a return to love, mercy, and humility—the heart of God's commandments. This prophetic courage set a foundation for Jesus' followers, challenging them to live out their faith authentically, even in the face of opposition.

Jesus' authenticity in this regard was grounded in His fidelity to His Father's intent. When the Jews opposed the good work Jesus performed on the Sabbath, Jesus said, "The Son can do nothing on his own, but only what he sees the Father doing" (John 5:19). Jesus' every act of commission and speech reflected the Father's desire. Although Elijah could not experience the completely pristine communion that Jesus and the Father shared, Elijah maintained his prophetic integrity, delivering the divine message with the divine intent in mind.

Elijah and Modern Prophets

Today's prophets face similar choices to the ones Jesus and Elijah faced in their times. In a digitally connected society, the pressure of conforming to popular opinion and prevailing beliefs is easily amplified. So are the voices of critics and celebrated influencers, both in the church and in the larger public square. Today's scrupulous prophets can barely utter a word without anticipating blowback.

It is no wonder modern prophets—or those who feel called to speak truth to power within religious communities—often grapple with the temptation to align their messages with popular or politically convenient narratives instead of conveying the uncomfortable truths that spiritual growth and accountability require. Yet what these contemporary spiritual leaders are called to navigate is the very tension between societal expectations and the demands of divine truth.

As has been true for millennia, the prophetic mission requires courage, independence, and a deep commitment to ethical integrity. Where this integrity is concerned, much hangs in the balance, not only for today's church but for future generations. The commitment to prophetic integrity ensures that prophetic guidance is genuine and is offered for the sake of God's people—to lead them toward righteousness by mirroring the law and the prophets as fulfilled and embodied in God's Son.

The call of God places very real demands on the one who is called. Being commissioned to prophesy to God's people is

Look What the Wind Blew In (to Ahab's Court)

not an entrance into the limelight for fame's sake. Like Jesus and Aslan, who were not "safe" but good, not clawing for attention but willing to be known and exposed to opposition, Elijah accepted the sacred burden. He adhered to his mission and paid a price for his calling. Today's genuine prophets will do the same—for Jesus' sake, for His people's sake, and for the sake of His plan for our world. Every man and woman called by God to prophesy will pay the price—either for testifying faithfully in His name or for testifying falsely in their own.

Soul-Searching Questions

- How does Elijah's persistence in prayer (see James 5:17–18) inspire you to stand in an extraordinary situation? How might his example of formation in prayer, communion, and solitude help you find courage for whatever you are facing?
- Is there an "Ahab" for whom you seem to be, at best, an annoyance? How does the knowledge of your calling/gifting/purpose enable you to see past the seeming rejection and fathom what God is working through it?
- Take a moment to reflect deeply on the areas of your life that need revitalization. Identify any neglected passions (or callings/giftings/purposes) that might be draining your vitality. Consider practical steps to reignite your faith and motivation in those areas.

5

Knowing Where We're Going

Then the word of Yahweh came to him, saying, "Go away from here and turn eastward, and hide yourself by the brook Cherith, which is east of the Jordan. And it will be that you will drink of the brook, and I have commanded the ravens to sustain you there." So he went and did according to the word of Yahweh, for he went and lived by the brook Cherith, which is east of the Jordan. And the ravens were bringing him bread and meat in the morning and bread and meat in the evening, and he would drink from the brook.

1 Kings 17:2–6 LSB

The journey with God is not static but continually unfolding. Elijah understood change was integral to his calling, and he knew who was leading whom. So he actively listened for the cues to lead him along the path his Lord had in mind. Elijah openly wrestled with fear and uncertainty. However, his internal question, "Where do we go from here?" was more searching of God's heart than a statement of resignation or defeat.

The word *then*, which opens 1 Kings 17:2, denotes a pivotal moment of transition and divine intervention. This tiny word signals a mighty shift in the story's direction, a moment when a temporal sequence connects with a critical point in God's redemptive plan. The word *then* marks the moment subsequent to Elijah's confrontation with the powers. Now he is hidden from King Ahab and miraculously sustained by ravens. He has entered a season of isolation and dependence on God's provision. But his time by the brook is more than a pause; it is a crucial period of preparation for what comes next.

The word *then* points to the precision of God's timing. God's word to Elijah (and to us) comes neither early nor late but according to its own sacred rhythm. God's instructions arrive when we are prepared to receive and act on them, often after a period of testing or growth. In the context of 1 Kings 17, *then* does more than connect events; it is a theological statement about the reliability of God's guidance into the next chapter of our work and witness in the world. This assurance encourages us to trust His timing and remain attentive.

The Word of the Lord Comes and Manifests

Following the word *then*, we see "the word of Yahweh came to [Elijah]" (1 Kings 17:2 LSB). This onset of a divine message confirmed the dynamic nature of God's communication. More than a prelude, it declared that when God speaks, His words become reality. They are not static but vibrant and transformative, actively shaping circumstances and fulfilling promises.

This essential truth has important implications. The Hebrew verb *hāyāh* suggests a process of becoming, or coming into existence, so that God's words are not only spoken but actualized.[1] The God of Elijah is our God, and He speaks things into being. Much as He revealed His words to Elijah, Samuel, and other prophets who were called into God's council, He

Knowing Where We're Going

continues to speak to us today. Therefore, our challenge becomes our opportunity—to listen deeply, discern clearly, and respond obediently to the divine voice that promises not only guidance but transformation.

From the "Let there be" commands in Genesis through all God's intimate dealings in human history, what He declared has transcended intention and emerged as an active force of creation and transformation.[2] Elijah understood this power intimately. During Elijah's time of silence, isolation, and prayer, Gilead served as a crucible in which God's voice molded his spirit.[3] This was imperative, as his prophetic authority and credibility with his own people depended on his readiness to recognize God's voice.

Let's be mindful that the voice and words of God to us are as potent as they were in Elijah's life. God's word commands creation, directs history, and personalizes His guidance to us. But we are summoned to recognize this inner dialogue. Daniel Brendsel notes that "prayer is properly our word of response to the God who initiates the conversation."[4] The late Eugene Peterson wrote, "Prayer is never the first word; it is always the second word. God has the first word."[5] God has always spoken first (Genesis 1:3). Hence, the Shema begins with "Hear, O Israel" (Deuteronomy 6:4).

Brendsel explains that God "initiates the relational dialogue by means of his word. He calls his people to attention and speaks first, 'Hear, O my people, and I will speak' (Psalm 50:7)."[6] God has promised to speak, but unless we are attentive, we will not hear Him. When God spoke to His prophets, the fulfillment of His words was as certain as the sunrise. If God has spoken *anything* into your life, its unfolding is inevitable. It's not a matter of *if* but *when*.

Remember that the fulfillment of God's prophetic word to Elijah validated its authenticity. According to Deuteronomy 18:22, if a prophet claims to speak on God's behalf, and that word is not fulfilled, then it is invalid, the Lord did not say it, and the prophet spoke presumptuously. This criterion for the genuineness of prophetic speech is inseparable from what Jeremiah 23:18 says about the council of Yahweh. I contend that in order for prophets from Moses to Malachi to prophesy what came to pass, they had to have entered the divine council to see and hear God's word.

As you make your spiritual journey, may you find an infusion of the Spirit's strength in the certainty of God's Word. Whether you are facing a period of uncertainty or standing on the threshold of a promise, remember the word of the Lord will surely come to pass. It is more than a promise; it is a presence that shapes reality, guides your steps, and confirms His faithfulness.

Moved by God's Word

After Elijah's bold confrontation with King Ahab, God instructed Elijah to depart and hide by the brook Cherith, believed to have been in Gilead. This territory was potentially familiar to Elijah and may have offered him seclusion and relative comfort during his isolation.[7] For a man separated from society once again and awaiting God's further directives, a known landscape could have evoked for Elijah a deep connection to the Promised Land and God's corresponding covenant. It was a place where he could navigate with a certain ease, finding a sense of balance and peace in the beautiful quietude that Gilead offered.

Such an environment could also have fostered for Elijah a sense of liminality—of being on the threshold between his past actions and the next phase of his prophetic mission. During his waiting and preparation, Elijah's hideout ultimately became his sanctuary. The solitude of the brook Cherith seems to offer a fitting context for communion with God, reinforcing Elijah's resolve and readiness for what was to come.

Knowing Where We're Going

The Hebrew name *Cherith* suggests themes of seclusion, provision, and transition. Verb and noun forms of the word derive from the root *karar*, which involves notions of circling, enclosing, accumulating, and separation.[8] These ideas resonate with Elijah's experience by the brook. It was a place of circular, protective boundaries that also accumulated and provided for his needs during his isolation.[9]

I see Cherith as more than a physical location in Elijah's journey. There, he discovered a place that accommodated his physical seclusion and further preparation. For us, Cherith is a metaphor that resonates with our own experiences. At times, we too seek refuge from our usual environments and routines. We might take a sabbatical from social media or practice the kind of silent prayer that goes all the way back to ancient Jewish and Christian customs. It might mean carving out a time to separate from the day's distractions to focus on personal growth and spiritual renewal. Whatever our purposeful seclusion looks like, it is our brook Cherith.

This Cherith experience is important in an increasingly transient, fast-paced, and often unreliable world. We search for clarity and for truths that are certain, just as people in Elijah's time did. Theirs was a similarly turbulent era, and Israel was a nation with a volatile history. Enduring was difficult enough; thriving was more so and required a significant emotional resilience and self-regulation. Elijah had to cultivate these qualities. They were essential to his story, and to Israel's.

Finding Flow and Embracing *Kairos*

God chose the gentle babble of the brook Cherith to separate Elijah from the deafening currents of injustice and false rhetoric surrounding the Northern Kingdom's court prophets. Cherith's sounds contrasted with the clamor of false prophecy and its effect on the masses. Elijah needed a temporary space of renewal and provision as the drought began to take its full effect. Eventually, the brook would dry up. But in this sacred space ordained by God for His prophet, its therapeutic qualities—its soft murmurs and flowing waters—soothed Elijah and broke the silence of the surrounding wilderness. There he found physical sustenance, serenity, solitude, and reflection.

When Elijah first arrived at Cherith, the brook was likely teeming with life. The banks of Elijah's safe haven also harbored birds and other creatures. The immediate environment was vibrant with biodiversity, mirroring the spiritual vitality such retreats offer. I believe the brook's sound was especially significant. Its continuous babble soothed Elijah and could remind him of God's constant presence. As such features do, it was able to touch the depths of his consciousness, allowing his heart to hear what God was speaking.

The essential solitude of Cherith invited Elijah to become attuned to God and commune with Him, as he was called to do. With every ripple and splash of the stream, Elijah could unwind and be drawn into listening for what wanted to emerge (John 16:13). In Scripture, streams often reveal what the flow of life is intended to be—a ceaseless stream of renewal and refreshment. Just as the waters flow unendingly, so too life is intended to move forward, always rejuvenating itself and offering new chances for growth and transformation.

At Cherith, Elijah did not merely pass the time. He was deeply immersed in *kairos*—the opportune, divine moment unlike the ordinary, sequential passage of time known as *chronos*. In chronos, time ticks by in a predictable, measurable way. It is marked by routine and often taken for granted. But in kairos, time expands and deepens. Its flowing moments are filled by God's transformative presence, purpose, and possibility. In kairos, time is not measured by hours or days but by spiritual significance and depth of experience. Time expands, deepens,

Knowing Where We're Going

and invites a turning inward, allowing Elijah to contemplate what is eternal and transcendent.

This chronos/kairos distinction was crucial for Elijah, as it is for us. The brook's rhythmic flow reminded him that God's providence and guidance are not bound by human measures of time but are revealed in moments when heaven touches earth. I believe this sacred pause attuned Elijah's attention to the history-making words that later emerged in the stillness. This waiting in the divine pauses prepared him for the further unfolding of God's eternal narrative.

Think about how timely Elijah's obedient retreat to Cherith was. He followed God's directive at the critical moment in his prophetic ministry, immediately preceding the drought's most destructive interval. By obeying God's command, Elijah ensured his survival and prepared for future challenges. Recognizing and responding to divine timing was essential to his future and the future of God's people.

Elijah's experience at Cherith was not only *timely* but amazingly *timeful*. As he remained by the brook, he lived fully in each moment and received his necessary provision—not only physical sustenance but the essential lessons he learned through his solitude and dependency on God. Each day testified to living in the present, listening attentively to God's voice, and being shaped by the experiences He provided. Elijah's sojourn at Cherith also tapped in to what is *timeless*—the eternal truths and divine principles that transcend temporal existence. His reliance on God reinforced the eternal truths of divine provision and protection. It proved the enduring principle that God cares for His own and will make a way for them, even in the most dire circumstances.

This truth has comforted believers throughout the ages and encouraged them to trust in God's unchanging character. Jennie Wilson's song "Hold to God's Unchanging Hand" reminds us that time and earth are subject to God.[10] His unchanging hand can be trusted above all else. Like Elijah at Cherith, we can navigate life's challenges and engage with time in the three dimensions of engaging with God: divine guidance, present awareness, and eternal perspective.

Redeeming the Kairos

Engaging with God presumes a state of conscious awareness. However, we are prone to periods of living on autopilot, which is antithetical to engaging with God. Saint Paul's exhortation, "Sleeper, awake! Rise from the dead" and renew the kairos because "the days are evil," resonates with the complexities of the current culture (Ephesians 5:14, 16). The passage encourages us to shift away from the slumber of complacency and the inertia of our routines. It urges us to become alert and aware of the divinely appointed kairos moments in which transformation and renewal in the flow of God's purposes become possible.

In a world buzzing with distractions, the noise of chronos (our everyday time) can drown out the subtle call of kairos' flow. As the ambient consumer-driven culture rushes forward, we find ourselves driven toward what is temporal and transient. Amid the rush, however, the Spirit of God offers a counterintuitive path, inviting us into the quiet, consistent flow of kairos and freeing us to cooperate with what wants to unfold. This is about more than finding peaceful moments; it is about actively participating in the transformation of our lives and our world. By stepping into the flowing kairos stream, we engage with the Spirit in a creative and dynamic partnership, and we become attentive to the movements of God's grace. Here, the potential to effect real change is present—the potential to shift paradigms and heal brokenness in subtle but historic ways.

Saint Paul suggests that to redeem the kairos is to consciously rise from the deadness of our daily routines and recognize the

Knowing Where We're Going

significance of the present moment—not as a tick of the clock but as an opportunity infused with eternity. It means discerning the times, understanding the deeper currents of God's actions, and responding to them with courage and faith. Living within kairos moments requires a vision that sees beyond the immediate, perceives the eternal in the mundane, and recognizes its transformative power when it is offered up in service to God.

In practical terms, this might look like choosing silence over noise, allowing ourselves regular periods of reflection and prayer despite our busy schedules, or responding to a call to serve those in need around us. It could involve advocating for justice where there is oppression, speaking truth where there is deception, or simply extending kindness where discord exists. When guided by the Spirit, these choices participate in the unfolding of God's redemptive work in the world.

As our world seems to grow darker with division, unrest, and moral ambiguity, the call to awaken and renew the kairos becomes ever more urgent. It is a call to align ourselves, not with the despair of the age but with the hope and transformative power of God's eternal kingdom. In this way, each believer and community of faith becomes a conduit of divine change, subtly but surely altering the course of history in the quiet strength of God's appointed time.

Redemption, Divine Streams, and True Identity

We can explore the idea of redemption through something the sons of Korah expressed in Psalm 46. They begin by describing God as a refuge and strength who is "abundantly available for help" in "tight places" (Psalm 46:1 NASB).[11] I suspect that once Elijah told King Ahab that he (Elijah) would control the rainfall, he found himself in a very tight place. There is great peril in having ruthless monarchs as enemies, and Elijah knew it. Ahab's wife Jezebel had ordered the execution of many prophets, and

Elijah's claim of authority over the weather placed him squarely in her (and Ahab's) sights.

Elijah found himself in a tight place, but his situation would be redeemed. The sons of Korah knew about tight places, and Psalm 46 captures elements of their history. The psalm's imagery is dramatic, with mountains slipping into the heart of the sea as though an earthquake had occurred. For the sons of Korah, such an event was all too real. They knew about their ancestor, who (with Dathan and Abiram) challenged God and Moses and was swallowed by the earth (Numbers 16:1–3, 31–32). The catastrophe's legacy was sobering for all of Korah's subsequent generations. It surely influenced the portrayal of natural upheaval in Psalm 46.

Yet through the psalm, the sons of Korah move from the turmoil of the earth to the tranquility of flowing water, writing, "There is a river whose streams make glad the city of God" (Psalm 46:4 NASB). This river symbolizes the life-giving work of the Holy Spirit. Although it is one river, it branches into many streams that represent the diverse expressions and ministrations of the Spirit that nourish the city and bring joy. Much the way William James vividly described consciousness as a flowing stream, this imagery describes the divine stream of consciousness that can be likened to the brook Cherith's flow.[12]

Cherith is an apt metaphor for a grace-filled stream of consciousness—a sacred space for deep reflection and introspection where Elijah could contemplate his identity and purpose. Proverbs 27:19 states, "Just as water reflects the face, so one human heart reflects another." In the brook's tranquil setting, Elijah could peer into the depths of his own heart and consider his own soul in light of the truths God revealed. The prophet could face himself fully while contemplating his fears, strengths, and the divine mandate upon his life.

This kind of reflective process is emblematic of the introspective journey we all are called to make. Away from the distractions

Knowing Where We're Going

of daily life, we can find our most profound encounters with God, and the Spirit can invite us to discover aspects of our true selves that we have not fully known. With His guidance, we can confront our deepest doubts and highest callings. Perhaps God often seeks to lead us into such places—not as punishment or abandonment, but as divine preparation in which the nudges of the Spirit, and not the tumult of our surroundings, shape us.

For us, Cherith can represent a spiritual crossing point where the noise of external identities and expectations yields to the clarity of divine calling and personal realization. There, the streams of God's grace can refresh us, allowing us to see ourselves as we truly are and align our lives with the reflection of God's purposes.

In Elijah's time of reflection, we see how our shortcomings can invite us to seek the Lord. Only He can anchor us in the understanding and acceptance of who we are in His eyes. We need this anchoring to deal with the *provisional self* or *selves* we tend to develop. The provisional self is the mask we wear to shape how others perceive us. While our provisional self can serve important purposes, it can also obstruct genuine intimacy with God and others. Therefore, it hinders our overall well-being and participation in the divine nature. At Cherith-like places of reflection, God calls us to shed our provisional selves and embrace our true-to-God identities. This deepens our intimacy with Him and moves us toward spiritual wholeness.

Cherith can also shift us from our tendency to politicize everything. At Cherith, Elijah became detached from the flow of falsehoods in the Northern Kingdom and could absorb insights and perspectives that were previously obscured. In Cherith-like places, we gain renewed perspectives of what the kingdom of Christ is really about and how Christ empowers us for mission. In a world torn by culture wars and politicization, we can perceive and embrace the expansion of the gospel that supersedes all politics.

Getting the Rhythm

Attuned to the rhythm of Cherith's waters, Elijah could learn the cadence of God's kingdom. Jesus promises the Spirit of truth will guide us into all truth and reveal what is to come (John 16:13). Intentionally stepping back from the noise of everyday life creates the space we need to perceive what the Spirit is telling us. As it did for Elijah, the separation for renewal equips us with fresh vision and aligns us more fully with the rhythm of grace and truth that God intends for our lives.

The deliberate adjustment to the kingdom's quiet, consistent tempo can allow the spirit of Elijah—"the essential principle" that animated him[13]—to be cultivated within us, increasing our awareness of the divine presence. In Pentecostal thought, when we employ the term "the spirit of Elijah," from Malachi 4:5–6 and from Zechariah's reiteration of the same in Luke 1:17, we are referring to a prophetic and transformative force that calls the people of God to repentance, preparing the way for the coming(s) of the Lord. In other words, while this does include the Second Coming, there are also in the "move of God" many "comings of the Lord" in church history, such as renewal movements, times of refreshing, times of revival, etc. that operate with boldness and supernatural power. It is that animating principle so evident in Elijah and emphasized canonically by Malachi and Zechariah, the father of John the Baptist (who, as Jesus made clear, was indeed the Elijah to come on the descent from the Mount of Transfiguration), that seeks to restore right relationships, confront idolatry, and ignite spiritual revival. Ultimately, the spirit of Elijah represents a deep connection between the prophetic role of Elijah in Scripture and the ongoing mission of the church as it anticipates the "comings" of the Lord by the Spirit and the ultimate return of Christ, along with the work to spread the gospel in the power of the Holy Spirit.

Knowing Where We're Going

As Christians, then, our fundamental approach is to behold God and perceive what He is up to. For those of us who are called as prophets, we can then relay to His people what needs to be done. And when the rest of us are prompted to encourage others, we can speak from what we have seen and heard in Him. Elijah's life revealed a prophetic stream of consciousness rooted in his awareness of the divine presence. He cultivated a prophetic perception attuned to God's voice, heart, and intentions. Such perception is crucial for prophetic consciousness that not only foresees events but understands the spiritual realities that underlie our visible circumstances. This was something of which Elijah was well aware.

Cherith's flow symbolizes the spiritual renaissance that renewed Elijah's capacity to perceive and participate in the divine flow. Beyond receiving revelations or insights, he participated in the life of the Spirit, whose rhythms shaped his own thoughts, actions, and responses. Elijah's time at Cherith further shaped his prophetic consciousness in ways that exceeded his survival needs. It recalibrated his spiritual senses to the divine frequency, so that each ripple of the water could evoke the deeper currents of God's purposes. Elijah emerged from this period not only physically sustained but spiritually acclimated to his calling and the challenges ahead. The experience finely honed his prophetic perception, enabling him to proceed with increased clarity and power.

The interplay of solitude, natural rhythm, and prophetic perception underscores how spiritual environments guide us into deeper participation in God's work in the world, as they also shape our capacity to hear God and enable us to respond to Him.

What's in a Name?

Hebrew names are revealing. Remember, the name *Cherith* denotes cutting and separation, among other things. Elijah could certainly attest to that! While he was at the brook, he experienced a literal and figurative cutting away from the prevailing societal norms, idol worship, and other corrupt practices that were rampant under Ahab and Jezebel.

Elijah's stay at Cherith was essential to his continuing in ministry and life. This required the cutting away of internal hindrances, a critical practice for Elijah and anyone seeking to embody the peaceable kingdom of God. Just as Elijah was cut off from the apostate society in order to be sustained by God alone, followers of Christ are called to a separation from the practices, systems, and ideologies that contradict the teachings and ethics of Christ and His kingdom. This separation is not a physical withdrawal from the world but a deliberate and discerning distancing of oneself from any values and behaviors that oppose wholeness and peace—the shalom Jesus embodied and preached during His earthly walk.

Brook Cherith experiences challenge us to examine the culture's pervasive narratives and power structures and recognize how sharply they conflict with the kingdom's radical peace. They invite us as the church to assess our engagement with matters of power and politics, and they urge a corporate and individual return to the Christlike ways of humility, service, and sacrificial love. These types of assessments paved Elijah's path forward at a critical point in his ministry. Just as Cherith sustained him for the longer term and prepared him to face the difficulties ahead, the spiritual discipline of separation can prepare and sustain us today, enabling us to live out the true essence of the gospel in a fractured world.

Allow and Permit

Knowing where we're going is less about intellectual decision-making and more about discerning God and His will as we go. We have explored how the imagery of a brook flowing effortlessly through the landscape serves as a powerful metaphor

Knowing Where We're Going

for the flow of divine grace and providence through our lives. Just as the earth's contours and boundaries guide the brook's flow, the divine influence moving through our lives is shaped by the circumstances and situations we encounter. Like the natural flow of a stream, divine movements do not require human propulsion; they are driven by forces much greater than any we could provide.

In the context of Elijah at the brook Cherith and our spiritual lives, the metaphorical lesson is astounding but simple. Our primary role is not to create or force the flow but to recognize, respond, and cooperate with it. This is less about taking charge and more about allowing God's will to manifest in and through us as we surrender to the currents He has set in motion, much the way a stray leaf trusts the flow of a stream to carry it.

This posture of allowing and permitting is based on trust and humility, requiring us to trust God has a direction and purpose for us even when neither seems apparent or comfortable. And it requires the humility to admit we do not control the universe and cannot possess more than a limited understanding of what is best.

In practical human responses, this posture means cultivating an attitude of attentive receptivity. When we pray, we do well to listen more than we speak. In our actions, we can observe more and assert ourselves less. We benefit from seeking to align our wills not with what seems best to us but with what God is already doing around us (John 5:19). This approach is not passive; it is a form of active engagement with spiritual discernment. It asks us to perceive the Holy Spirit's subtle invitations, recognizing the opportunities placed before us to act justly, love mercy, and walk humbly (Micah 6:8).

Cooperating with the flow of the Spirit also means being willing to release our preconceptions and need for control. It might mean stepping into unknown situations with faith. Or it could involve staying in places of uncertainty while trusting God's timing for change. For Elijah, it meant staying by the brook until the word came to move. Each day, as Elijah depended on ravens and a dwindling water supply, his understanding of reliance and divine provision deepened. He became less driven and more willing to be led.

Elijah's experience at the brook Cherith encourages us to cultivate a spirituality that respects the natural flow of divine grace through our lives, teaching us that our greatest strength is often found in our willingness to surrender, and our most effective actions are those that move with the greater currents of God's purposeful activity in the world.

Soul-Searching Questions

- Reflecting on your spiritual journey, what are some ways you might cultivate a keener awareness of life's *kairos* moments? When have you best embraced seasons of flow and alignment with God's purposes? How did you respond with faith and perseverance to face obstacles or setbacks at those times?

- How can the experiences you just described help you to further nurture spiritual growth and the development of godly character traits such as responsibility and integrity?

- How can you cultivate a heightened awareness of the kairos moments in your spiritual journey? What practices or disciplines can help you discern the opportune times when God is inviting you to step out in faith, embrace a new challenge, or deepen your character and integrity?

- In what areas of your life are you currently experiencing a sense of flow or alignment with God's purposes? How can you lean into the flow? How might this help to propel you forward with renewed commitment in your spiritual journey?

6

Fed by Dirty Birds

The word of the LORD came to him, saying, "Go away from here and turn eastward, and hide yourself by the brook Cherith, which is east of the Jordan. It shall be that you will drink of the brook, and I have commanded the ravens to provide food for you there." So he went and did according to the word of the LORD, for he went and lived by the brook Cherith, which is east of the Jordan. The ravens brought him bread and meat in the morning and bread and meat in the evening, and he would drink from the brook.

1 Kings 17:2–6 NASB

Expect the Unexpected

Elijah's extraordinary experience at the brook Cherith seems tailored by God to be unforgettable. God chose to provide for His weary prophet in a manner as unexpected as it was miraculous and as unconventional as it was divine. Ravens—scavengers typically regarded as unclean according to the law and selfish by nature—were commanded by God to feed Elijah. Twice a day, these unlikely servants brought him bread and meat. For ravens, sharing was no ordinary occurrence. Yet in obedience to God's command, they delivered Elijah's sustenance every morning and evening.

This remarkable method of provision draws us to a stunning truth about God's nature. His resources are boundless, and His methods are not confined by human understanding or societal norms. God unmistakably displayed His sovereignty over creation as these birds (usually symbols of desolation and loneliness) became messengers of provision and survival. The regularity of this provision underscored Elijah's daily dependence on God. Much as the manna that fell from heaven and fed the Israelites in the wilderness, Elijah's food could not be stored. It was provided anew each day and served as a lesson in trust. Elijah could not hoard or save food, but had to live in the faith that God's provision would come again tomorrow.

God's way of sustaining Elijah required certain adjustments in his psychological and spiritual understanding. Firmly rooted in the notions of purity and impurity delineated in Leviticus 11:15 and Deuteronomy 14:14, Elijah had to reassess his preconceptions and broaden his understanding of God's sovereignty. Being fed by dirty birds forced him to realize God's methods often defy human expectations.

Fast-forward over three millennia to the present. Our lives bear little resemblance to Elijah's rugged existence. In our lingo, the expression *eat crow* suggests not a menu selection but a bitter humiliation. It is hard to imagine the ravens delivered bread fresh from someone's oven. Surely, bakers and butchers were scarce in the wilderness. Perhaps the ravens pilfered bread from a far-off encampment. And the meat they delivered might well have been leftovers they scavenged from a predator's feast. Elijah's meal might not pass modern health inspections, but it sustained him—not only with nutritional value but through the faith the meal represented.

God's provision often comes in unexpected forms from improbable sources. For Elijah, God required a season in the school of the Spirit during which he learned to accept God's grace as it was given rather than as he would have chosen. We might chuckle and even recoil at the thought of eating what Elijah ate. But his experience reminds us that no matter how God delivers, His provision perfectly meets our needs.

Elijah's experience puts a new spin on "eating crow"! Instead of humiliation, the prophet encountered humility, dependence, and acceptance of God's ways. Elijah was entirely at the Lord's mercy. He had no backup plan or stores of food. Elijah was painfully aware of his vulnerability and absolute dependence on God. His experience at the brook Cherith took Elijah beyond a theoretical belief in divine provision and transformed his faith into a tangible, lived reality. The shift from conceptual faith to experiential trust radically deepened his spiritual journey and emphasized not only God's ability to provide but also His intimate involvement in His prophet's life. For Elijah, every delivered meal was a spiritual signpost of God's faithfulness and care.

The ravens' twice-daily visits also altered Elijah's perception of God's interaction with nature. Observing birds, typically scavengers, acting against their natural instincts to feed Elijah reinforced his awareness of God's omnipotence and direct involvement in the natural world. This recognition might shift Elijah's understanding of God from a deity who occasionally intervenes to one who is intimately and constantly involved in the workings of the world He created.

The Ravens Tell a Story

At this point in the Elijah narrative, the ravens are center stage, making their resilience relevant to us. Remember that Jesus talked about these remarkable birds and summoned us to consider their nature:

> Consider the ravens: they neither sow nor reap, they have neither storehouse nor barn, and yet God feeds them. Of how much more value are you than the birds! And can any of you by worrying can add a single hour to your span of life? If then you are not able to do so small a thing as that, why do you worry about the rest?
>
> Luke 12:24–26

By pointing to the ravens in relation to divine provision, Jesus invites us to marvel at God's way of caring for His creations— even lowly scavengers. Despite the ravens' inability to harvest or store their food, they lack nothing for their survival. This was not an idle fact Jesus added to a sermon. He was speaking to the lives of human beings whose trust in God is sometimes shaken.

Remember what happened when the flood was over and Noah wondered whether it was safe to leave the ark. "At the end of forty days Noah opened the window of the ark . . . and sent out the raven; and it went to and fro until the waters were dried up from the earth" (Genesis 8:6–7). The raven's role in the flood account illustrates the bird's adaptability and independence. When Noah released the raven, it did not return to the ark. Obviously, the creature was capable of sustaining itself in the flood's aftermath by relying on its scavenging instincts, even amid mass devastation.

The raven's behavior after its release points to God's provision amid desolation. Unlike the dove that returned with an olive branch, the fact the raven did not return indicates its ability to thrive independently, with resilience being part of God's good creation. The bird's independence might also symbolize a divine sustenance that is continuous and omnipresent, even when not directly observable.

Fed by Dirty Birds

The raven's story is linked to Elijah's experience because the creature that managed to survive after the flood later became a vessel of sustenance for Elijah. There is a sense of continuity that showcases the raven's unique ability to function both independently and as an instrument of divine intervention for Elijah. Let's consider this in relation to deep listening and discernment. The Elijah narrative contains insights into the capabilities and spiritual significance ravens carry. I believe these insights will shed light on the ravens' interaction with Elijah and on the larger theme of this book.

Resilience in God's Good Creation and in Elijah's Life

Ravens are remarkably adaptable and resilient, able to thrive in varied and often harsh environments according to the intricate design of God's creation. Ravens are found across the globe, from desert lands to arctic habitats, and they have an uncommon capacity to find food where little exists. This aspect of their resilience is about more than their survival instincts; it presses the point that the Creator who equips even the least of His creatures surely equips us.

Much the way their independence does, the ravens' resilience in Scripture serves as a metaphor for God's provision. The ravens that served Elijah relied on the environment God provided. Likewise, we are called to trust in God's provision for us. Their daily lives—devoid of sowing or reaping yet full of God's provision (Luke 12:24–26)—remind us of the Father's promise to meet our needs according to His riches in glory (Philippians 4:19).

This reliance on God is not born of naïveté. It stems from a foundational awareness of our place as image-bearers in God's world (Genesis 1:26–28). The ravens don't worry about their next meal; they simply live within the means their Creator provides. Especially in our moments of doubt and need, the ravens' behavior urges us to remember who we are in God's eyes, realizing we are even more valuable than the birds, and His care and provision are assured.

The ravens' resilience naturally brings us back to Elijah, his experience at Cherith, and what occurred inside him. The ravens were not just delivering food; they embodied God's promise to sustain and nourish His servants, thus intertwining the natural resilience of His creation with the supernatural provision for His people. Therefore, the bond between Elijah and the ravens reminds us to live free from worry. Especially in moments of doubt and need, we need to remember who we are in God's eyes. We are much more valuable than the birds, and He assures us of His care and provision.

From a psychological standpoint, Elijah's protective isolation, coupled with the unconventional means of his survival, could foster the significant growth of spiritual resilience. His isolation at Cherith necessitated a deeper inner fortitude and sense of resolve. He was positioned to cultivate a resilience rooted not in his own strength but in his reliance on God.

Let's consider how that is different from common views of resilience. The term *resilience* has gotten a lot of play since the COVID-19 pandemic. Publications in fields such as health, psychology, education, and corporate leadership refer to it often.[1] The *American Psychological Association Dictionary* describes resilience as "the process and outcome of successfully adapting to difficult or challenging life experiences, especially through mental, emotional, and behavioral flexibility and adjustment to external and internal demands."[2]

Essentially, that definition describes something we need to learn to do: bounce back from adversity, stress, and even tragedy. The focus is on our personal capabilities, our psychological strengths, and the social environments in which we live, as we will see. The idea is that human resilience is developed through our life experiences, education, and environment and typically

Fed by Dirty Birds

focuses on two things: our internal resources and our external support systems.

Mind you, there are multiple components that impact how well or poorly we adapt to challenges, setbacks, and adversities. Among them are:

1. The ways in which we see, interpret, and interact with the world
2. The social resources that are available to us
3. The coping strategies we employ[3]

Now let's examine these three more closely.

How We See, Interpret, and Interact with the World

Our very individual approaches in this regard remind me of the famous quote by the late Cuban American writer Anaïs Nin. "We do not see things as they are, we see them as we are."[4] Each person views their surroundings and interacts with the world uniquely. Why? Because our perceptions are colored by our personal experiences, beliefs, cultural heritage, cherished values, momentary emotions, and other inner states (our personal subjectivity). These factors shape our sense of reality and therefore our way of interpreting it.

For example, our emotional state influences our perceptions. When joy fills our heart, we see the world in a brighter light. Conversely, in times of sorrow or distress, the world can appear dimmer, and challenges might seem more daunting. Similarly, our cultural backgrounds inform our interactions. What seems respectful or appropriate in one culture may be an affront in another, affecting our relationships and communications. Moreover, our deeply held values and beliefs act as filters, coloring our interactions and choices in subtle but profound ways.

Understanding these factors and our overall subjectivity can foster empathy and compassion and draw us together. When we consider other people's perspectives and question our own assumptions, we can remain open to learning from experiences different from our own. This helps us to recognize and set aside our biases, see beyond the boundaries of our personal views, and embrace a broader, more inclusive vision of the world.

As we journey with Christ, we are ever called to see the world through His eyes—eyes that offer grace, understanding, and love. By doing so, we can transform not only our perspectives but also our relationships, communities, and even our own hearts. Our prayers in this regard need to be rooted in listening for and discerning the wisdom of Christ in order that we might see more clearly and love more deeply, remembering always that our unique views of the world continually need to be renewed by the transformative power of God's Spirit within us.

The Availability and State of Social Resources

When it comes to what psychological research suggests about the accessibility and caliber of social resources, we want to be as wise as serpents and harmless as doves. God provides social resources to enrich our lives and deepen our journey with Him and one another. We must navigate the complexities of engaging with these resources in a postmodern, post-Christian era, recognizing that although various networks and community assets are valuable, we need to approach them with caution and discernment.

Our relationships with family, friends, church members, or colleagues form the core of our social support. These bonds offer us emotional and spiritual sustenance, echoing the interconnectedness Christ desires. However, when we extend our engagement to broader community services, including those provided by governmental and nongovernmental organizations,

Fed by Dirty Birds

we need to discern how these sources align with our values and beliefs. As followers of Jesus, we are not called to blindly accept what the world offers. When we participate in community services, educational institutions, and professional networks, we need also to maintain our core values and not absorb influences uncritically. At the same time, balancing our involvement does not mean withdrawing into echo chambers that stifle our perspectives and growth. Either error can lead us away from our faith principles.

In our digital age of abundant and often unfiltered information, the challenge is even greater. Online communities and networks can provide remarkable opportunities to connect and fellowship. But they require us to discern the information we consume and share. It is crucial we do not isolate ourselves among those who see the world exactly as we do. It is equally important, however, that we are mindful of our information sources and carefully vet them.

Our local churches can help to ground us as we serve and are served, as we learn and teach, and as we grow in faith and help others to do the same. We can foster a culture of openness mixed with discernment, creating safe spaces for dialogue and learning. May we not ignore any spiritual abuse of authority, sexual abuse, consumer-driven theologies, and compromises of the sacred text. These toxins fragment the church and leave it in need of renewal.

Before we talk about coping strategies, let's delve a little deeper into the topic of resources.

Elijah Was a Loner

First, let's note a striking aspect of Elijah's character: his solitude. For all intents and purposes, he was what we might call a loner. This loner status was not only a personal choice but an essential element of his prophetic calling that influenced how he interacted with the world around him. I propose from a context of a Christ-centered perspective that this way of life was Elijah's cross to bear.

Elijah's loner status is integral to understanding his resilience and his reliance on divine provision, particularly during his isolation on Cherith's banks. He, the brook, and the ravens reveal aspects of divine providence for a man who carried a history-making, earth-shaking word in his time. In the context of his broader prophetic journey, solitude was not just a backdrop but a crucial component of Elijah's spiritual strength and resilience, orchestrated by God.

After his confrontation with Ahab, Elijah was no longer a solitary prophet. Instead, he became a marked man, and he carried the weight of national destiny. His seclusion was strategic and necessary for continuing his mission while under threat from the reigning powers. He was far from isolated in spirit; he was deeply enmeshed in the spiritual struggle for Israel's soul. His seclusion was a period of intense inner wrestling, not for personal sanctuary but for intercession and preparation for what lay ahead.

I believe that in this phase, Elijah's prophetic integrity was crucial. He stood as an uncompromising voice against Ahab and Jezebel's efforts to align Israel with the surrounding idolatrous nations. Elijah's resistance and resilience were a testament to his deep passion for Yahweh's glory, passion he maintained regardless of personal risk. Throughout his seclusion, Elijah bore the nation's compromise and spiritual adultery on his heart and maintained a posture of utter submission to the God who calls His people to covenantal faithfulness. Elijah carried the burden of prophetic truth in a time of national crisis, and his life reflected the cost of his prophetic integrity: specifically, the personal sacrifices he made in the pursuit of divine justice and the restoration of Israel's faith.

Elijah's absence did not detract from his mission. His withdrawal from the courts of Ahab and Jezebel only intensified the witness of his previous presence. Like Moses, who spent forty years in seclusion before returning to Egypt to dismantle Pharaoh's oppressive empire, Elijah's period of hiddenness signified the prophetic tradition that existed from Moses to Malachi, and it revealed a life set apart for God and His burden.

Not everyone is called to carry the mantle of prophetic burden or live in such extreme solitude. Some might find their walk with God involves seasons of solitude, but the faithfulness of many others will be expressed in community, family, or the non-isolation of urban ministry. While Moses' and Elijah's experiences were uniquely tailored to their God-given missions and callings, they are not a blueprint for every believer. Yet it behooves us to discern which lessons we might glean from Elijah's solitude. The key is in understanding the principles of faith, obedience, and justice that Elijah exemplified, and considering how they can inform our own journeys with God.

Although the scriptural narrative provides certain insights into Elijah's personal history, it leaves unanswered questions about his capacity for relationship building. In God's instructions to Elijah about anointing Elisha as his prophetic successor, we glimpse the beginning of an enduring but relationally complex partnership. Hints of the men's interactions suggest Elijah's formidable personality, including his stern resolve and intense focus on his divine mission. For Elisha, these traits probably posed interpersonal difficulties. This dynamic shaped Elisha in meaningful ways but also created a demanding mentoring situation marked by a complicated blend of temperaments.

The Divine Element in Resilience

The dynamics between Elijah and Elisha are not part of this study, but acknowledging the inherent challenges in mentoring relationships is. Elijah's intensity and demanding prophetic mission surely tested both his and Elisha's resilience. The resilience in this case (and ours) isn't about overcoming adversities through sheer will and determination, but rather about how divine guidance shapes our capacities so resilience surpasses human effort and becomes a transformative power that sustains and redefines our handling of difficulties. Just as Elisha's resilience was honed through Elijah's mentorship and the divine orchestration of the men's paths, our resilience can be refined by opening ourselves to God's involvement in our lives.

This divine influence does not diminish the role of human agency but rather enhances it, infusing our natural resilience with spiritual strength and wisdom. It invites us to view resilience not only as a survival mechanism but as a dynamic process of spiritual and emotional growth nurtured by personal struggles and encounters with the divine.

Divine resilience embodies the noticeable strength and steadfast endurance that emanate from a deepening faith, meticulously shaped and perfected in Elijah and us by the Spirit. Remember that ravens—creatures typically driven by instinct—defied their own nature to provide for the prophet. This miraculous anomaly is a life lesson about how divine provision transcends natural expectations. The rhythm and cadence of the God-sent ravens assures us of God's presence in every beginning and every conclusion, in the unfolding of each day, and in the closure of every chapter.

The ravens' resilience highlights Elijah's resilient faith in a God who imbued the creatures with unusual steadfastness and rendered their actions predictably miraculous. Their rhythmic morning-and-evening provision at the brook Cherith reflects God's ways. Their predictably miraculous cadence sustained Elijah and underscored a divine synchronicity perfectly aligned with the needs and season of Elijah's life. Such divine orchestration invites us to appreciate the nuances of God's interventions. They are not arbitrary but are intricately woven into the fabric of our circumstances and times. Although Elijah expected to see

Fed by Dirty Birds

God's hand in dramatic rescues and in life's almost mundane miracles, the miraculous was not a constant spectacle. It was a sacred alignment with God's timing and purposes. We are invited to trust in a dimension of God's care that transcends simple causality and enters the realm of divine synchronicity in which we find a deeper resonance with God's ways. Aligning ourselves with His will might not cause us to experience miracles in the conventional sense every day, but we will discern the miraculous in everyday situations—in the perfectly timed help, the unexpected provision, and the fresh strength that arrives in moments of great need. Elijah's story encourages us to cultivate a resilient faith that is both aware of and relying upon these divinely synchronized moments, trusting that God's presence is both mysterious and manifest, guiding us through every season of our lives.

From this divine vantage point, resilience is much more than enduring; it is about expecting the extraordinary amid the ordinary. Resilience develops in the crucible of trust, where we come to anticipate miraculous interventions and favorable outcomes in scenarios demanding more than human effort. Thus, divine resilience invites us to a higher plane of existence. From that vantage point, our daily reliance on God transforms our understanding of resilience and intertwines our spiritual fortitude with the miraculous. This is where the improbable becomes profoundly possible.

Reflection for Our Lives

Elijah's experience as a loner reveals how periods of isolation can serve as times of testing, as well as intended opportunities for divine encounter and personal transformation. The unique solitude that marked his prophetic ministry was necessary in shaping his deep communion with God, forging a deeper reliance on God, and equipping him for the difficult aspects of his calling. Understanding this can help us to embrace our solitary experiences as potential spaces of divine instruction and empowerment. While social resources are valuable, Elijah's story reminds us of the power of solitude to shape us into vessels suited for our unique purposes in God's plan.

The Coping Strategies We Employ

The American Psychological Association defines *coping strategies* as "actions, series of actions, or thought processes utilized in addressing stressful or unpleasant situations or in modifying one's reaction to such situations." While we often rely on a range of coping strategies, from problem-solving and seeking support to relaxation techniques and physical activity,[5] Elijah's example presents a model of resilience grounded in utter dependence on God. Because he lived a solitary life, Elijah's coping did not primarily involve the human-centered strategies with which we are familiar. Instead, his continuous reliance on God's provision and guidance sustained his resilience.

Particularly during his seclusion at the brook Cherith, Elijah's coping strategy (if it could be called that) was his unwavering faith. This is in stark contrast to the more active, problem-solving approaches that are popular today. Elijah's faith led him to embrace God's interventions as his primary source of support, with prayer and listening for God's voice serving as his principal techniques for managing stress. Instead of turning to human relationships, Elijah turned to God. This meant he had to adjust his expectations to God's purposes and embrace his circumstances as part of a larger divine plan. His prayer and communion with God were vital to his survival and the sharpening of his discernment. Elijah's physical movements—from one place of refuge to another—were acts of obedience that also served to strengthen him spiritually and emotionally.

Fed by Dirty Birds

Examining Elijah's solitary and God-dependent lifestyle can help us see how a deeper integration of faith can enhance our own coping strategies. Although not all are called to the extremes of Elijah's prophetic mission, incorporating elements of his divine reliance can expand our perspectives beyond the tangible, enrich our resilience, and make us more adept navigators of life's challenges.

Meat and Bread

The miraculous provision the ravens delivered to Elijah is not described in detail as to the specific types of bread and meat. Yet this does not diminish the semiotic richness of the story. Instead, it invites a deeper exploration of the items' symbolic and sacramental significance. The bread and meat are not mere sustenance; they are signs and symbols of divine provision and spiritual nourishment.

This dual provision parallels the account of quail and manna in Exodus 16. Just as God provided quail and manna (bread from heaven) to sustain the Israelites physically and affirm God's fidelity, the meat and bread God provided for Elijah reinforce the theme of His unfailing provision even in desolation. In his book *The Prophetic Imagination*, Walter Brueggemann offers this reflection on God's provision: "The counterculture of Moses lived in a world of scarcity, whether one talks about hurriedly eaten unleavened bread (Exodus 12:8–11) or the strange gift of manna from heaven in the wilderness (Exodus 16)."[6]

According to Brueggemann, these episodes challenge our common anxieties about scarcity. He invites us to rethink our views by reflecting on the God who meets us in our needs—not merely filling our emptiness but also transforming our understanding of what we truly need. Whether in the unleavened bread or in the manna, God did not merely sustain Israel. These provisions were (and are) symbols of God's promise and faithfulness. Each day, as the Israelites gathered their manna, they learned to depend not on their own supplies but on God's continuing faithfulness.

Invitation to Reframing

Brueggemann's reflections on God's provision evoke what I believe is essential as we examine Elijah's season of profound isolation. The text that describes the ravens' morning-and-evening deliveries illumines the transformative process that redefined his perception of those needs. This was a fundamental reframing for Elijah—a fundamental shift in how he perceived his circumstances, interpreted their significance, and responded to them. Elijah's story invites our reframing as well, to see beyond what is immediate and apparent, and instead embrace a deeper, faith-driven understanding of the situations we face.

Reframing is more than an adjustment of expectations; it is a radical overhaul of our conceptual framework that challenges us to question our assumptions about scarcity and prompts us to discover what we truly value and depend upon. In scriptural terms, this reframing is often driven by encounters with God that compel us to reconsider our definitions of necessity and sufficiency.

For example, in the wilderness, the Israelites had to learn to see manna not just as food but as a recurring reminder of God's presence and promise. Each flake of manna called them to trust in God's ongoing provision. Similarly, Elijah's sustenance by ravens was a lesson in the reliability of God's word and the importance of relying solely on Him.

The process of getting to faith, then, involves this essential reframe, requiring us to view our challenges and provision not just in terms of how they meet our physical needs but how they fulfill us spiritually and draw us closer to divine realities. When we begin to see our lives through this lens of faith, our responses move from anxiety and fear toward trust and

Fed by Dirty Birds

expectancy, knowing God is at work in ways we might not have anticipated.

This reframing leads to transformation, changing us from the inside out and affecting how we think and live. Reframing urges us to live in a state of open expectancy that keeps us looking for God to show up. It makes us always ready to see His hand in our daily bread and always prepared to find deeper meaning in our experiences. This transformation fosters a resilient faith that does not waver with circumstances but deepens with each divine encounter.

As we learn to reframe our situations through the lens of faith, we open ourselves to the transformative work of God. We become participants in a spiritual journey that continually shapes us into beings who are both sustained by God's provisions and deeply changed by them. Therefore, the reframing of our needs and responses becomes a pathway to a more enduring faith that is based on the certainty of God's unfailing love and provision.

God's provision in times of scarcity reveals God operates within a realm of divine abundance not defined by our definitions of lack or plenty. The ravens reveal the nature of God's provision in the liminal spaces—the in-between places where human need and divine provision intersect. God is neither moved by our abundance nor threatened by our lack. He is the God of the "already" and the "not yet," who meets us in our present uncertainties with assurances of His faithfulness. Whether our circumstances are characterized by plenty or by want, they are opportunities to experience the reality of God's kingdom, which operates on principles alien to a world that sees itself governed by scarcity.

Saint Paul learned this in his own life and in response to the call of God:

> Not that I am referring to being in need; for I have learned to be content with whatever I have. I know what it is to have little, and

I know what it is to have plenty. In any and all circumstances I have learned the secret of being well-fed and of going hungry, of having plenty and of being in need. I can do all things through him who strengthens me.

Philippians 4:11–13

Paul speaks of divine provision and contentment in words that also mirror Elijah's experiences. Paul speaks of an abiding inner peace, a contentment learned through abundance and scarcity. His reliance on Christ's strength to endure and thrive in every circumstance highlights a faith that transcends external conditions and is grounded in trust and dependency on God's sufficiency.

The parallel to Elijah's life is striking. When Elijah faced deprivation from the drought he himself prophesied, he and all Israel had to depend solely on God's provision. For the prophet, provision came through ravens, and no one else could see how God sustained him. Some of God's miracles are not for public consumption. They are signs to us personally, and they draw us further up and into communion with the triune God. Like Paul, Elijah learned to be content with God's provision. Both figures exemplified the graced spiritual resilience that flourishes not from earthly abundance but from an unwavering faith in God's presence and power.

Feeding on Christ

The provisions we have examined also prefigure Christ, who is humanity's ultimate sustenance. The bread Christ offers is Himself. He declared Himself "the bread of life" (John 6:35), signifying that no one who comes to Him would hunger. Feeding on Him sustains us through life's vicissitudes and offers spiritual sustenance that endures through all circumstances.

When the ravens brought bread to Elijah, it was part of a larger divine narrative. According to Revelation 13:8, Christ

Fed by Dirty Birds

is the "Lamb slain from the foundation of the world" (NKJV). This theological perspective, echoed in Isaiah 46:10, where God declares "the end from the beginning" (NKJV), suggests that all of creation, including the seemingly mundane provision of bread by ravens, is sanctified through Christ's eternal sacrifice. This sanctification was realized fully in the incarnation, when God sent His Son, and it imbues all elements of creation with divine significance. Therefore, the bread (as well as the meat) provided to Elijah—and indeed all acts of Providence—are part of the sanctified cosmos, transformed by Christ's sacrificial love. Through Him, the mundane is lifted into the realm of the sacred, making every act of provision an opportunity to connect with the God who made us for Himself.

Thus, Elijah's reliance on the ravens was participation in the cosmic sanctification wrought by Christ. From the meat, we can draw a parallel to Christ's teachings, often difficult and "meaty," requiring a mature palate trained in discernment—the discernment that Hebrews 5:14 associates with those who have their senses trained to discern good and evil. Here, the meat can be viewed as the deeper, more substantial doctrines of Christianity, requiring contemplation and a mature faith to be fully appreciated.

In the sacramental context, the narrative describing Elijah's provision at the brook Cherith encompasses the eucharistic imagery where bread and wine symbolize Christ's body and blood offered for the salvation of mankind. In this sacrament, believers partake of Christ's life (which is infused in the bread and the cup) and participate in mystical union with Him. The bread and the meat provided to Elijah can be seen as prefiguring this sacrament, where the physical act of eating and drinking points to a far deeper spiritual reality—the nourishment of our souls through Christ's sacrifice and the ongoing sustenance provided by God's Word.

The bread and meat provided to Elijah suggest layers of meaning that stretch across the canon of Scripture. They remind us of God's provision in our times of need; they point us to Christ as the source of our spiritual sustenance; and they invite us to partake of the richer and fuller teachings that shape our lives, deepen our communion with God, and enable us to listen, discern, and step forward.

Soul-Searching Questions

- In your view, what is the importance of resilience in the context of spiritual strength and the perseverance of faith? In what specific, practical ways can you cultivate resilience through your spiritual practices?
- Resilience is not just about bouncing back to where you were before adversity struck; it's also about bouncing beyond and growing from the experience. Consider how you might cultivate adaptive resilience. What role would your personal and spiritual growth play in its development?
- How can adaptive resilience enable you to expect the unexpected and embrace challenges as opportunities for personal and spiritual growth? What mindset shifts or perspectives are needed to view adversity as a catalyst for transformation, rather than just a hindrance or temporary setback?

7

Life in a Culture of Death

After a while the wadi dried up, because there was no rain in the land. Then the word of the LORD came to [Elijah], saying, "Go now to Zarephath, which belongs to Sidon, and live there; for I have commanded a widow there to feed you."

1 Kings 17:7–9

As we enter the story at 1 Kings 17:7, we witness a moment of crisis and deep spiritual reflection for Elijah. The reality could not be starker. There has been no rain in Israel, and even the brook Cherith has dried up. The drought is not a mere weather event but a divine judgment of the idolatrous practices Ahab and Jezebel forcefully promoted. Now the lack of rain has afflicted the land and the people, not only those who oppose Elijah's God but also those who are faithful to Him, including Elijah.

Everyone is experiencing the trials that befall a nation under divine scrutiny. Yet God directs Elijah to go Zarephath in Sidon, where a certain widow will feed him.

> So [Elijah] set out and went to Zarephath. When he came to the gate of the town, a widow was there gathering sticks; he called to her and said, "Bring me a little water in a vessel, so that I may drink." As she was going to bring it, he called to her and said, "Bring me a morsel of bread in your hand."
>
> 1 Kings 17:10–11

The widow's response is heavy with the sense of impending death. She and her son are about to eat a meager final meal, after which she fully expects they both will perish of starvation (v. 12). Elijah understands their plight. He had already experienced the effects of the drought at the brook Cherith. But now, he witnesses the impact on perfect strangers and experiences their plight in a very personal way, knowing he had essentially prophesied their present devastation.

The weight of this reality surely pressed deeply into Elijah's spirit. As he did at the brook Cherith, he faced not only the fallout of a physical drought but also the pain of a substantial spiritual and psychological trial. We have already seen that his period of isolation transcended mere physical survival and marked a pivotal deepening of his prophetic consciousness. Alone and vulnerable, he was compelled to confront the immense burden of responsibility he carried as a prophet of God. I believe the divine orchestration of events was designed to refine his understanding of his calling. God was not only testing Elijah's faith but also teaching him the delicate balance of power and humility intrinsic to authentic spiritual leadership.

Elijah's reliance on God intensified as he experienced first-hand God's severity and mercy—the severity in judgment as displayed through the drought, and the mercy as God directed him toward provision in Zarephath. Therefore, Elijah's journey from Cherith to Zarephath was not only geographic; it was a precarious spiritual passage from knowing about God's sovereignty to experiencing the terrifying beauty of it.

Elijah's stewardship of his prophetic role evolved significantly during this period. Each day brought a deeper understanding of the divine balance between judgment and grace, and each night unveiled a clearer revelation of his minuscule yet pivotal role in the vast narrative of God's interaction with humanity. In embracing his vulnerability and accepting his solitary path, Elijah was not weakened but strengthened. This solidifying of his prophetic authority did not come through displays of power but through Elijah's quiet, unyielding faith in his God.

History Never Happens in a Vacuum

Long before Elijah's time, after the great flood receded and humanity began to spread across the earth, the city of Sidon (of which Zarephath later became a part) emerged from the industriousness of Noah's grandson Sidon, the firstborn of Noah's son Canaan. This coastal city became a bustling hub of commerce, culture, and craftsmanship and swiftly grew into one of the earliest and most influential cities of the region. Its master navigators and traders sailed the known world in ships laden with cedar and luxury handicrafts. Their skill in navigation and trade made Sidon a city of wealth and sophistication.

In the days when Joshua led the Israelites into Canaan, Sidon fell within the allotment assigned to the tribe of Asher. However, the Israelites never fully subdued the fierce and proud Sidonians. Instead, Sidon remained a powerful and sometimes troublesome neighbor, a reminder that, in their quest to settle the Promised Land, the Israelites' interactions with local people groups would be necessarily complicated. Although Tyre eventually became the foremost Phoenician city, Sidon remained a crucial center of Phoenician culture, and the term *Sidonian* became synonymous with *Phoenician*.

Centuries later, the streets of Sidon witnessed the coming of new figures destined to leave their mark on history. Jesus

Himself traveled through Tyre and Sidon. Paul also visited the place, further entwining its story with the emerging narrative of Christianity. As Sidon grew into a place of encounter and exchange, sailors and prophets and kings and craftsmen played out their roles with the Mediterranean tides as their backdrop. Every detail of Sidon's recorded history was a testament to its place as a perpetual bridge between cultures and epochs.[1]

Despite Sidon's role in fostering connections, those made between Israel and Sidon were complicated and often paved with compromised intentions. Relationships between neighboring people groups in the ancient Middle East were rarely straightforward, and Israel's ties with Sidon certainly exemplify the region's complexity. Geopolitical interactions were not only adversarial; they were also deeply entwined with Israel's own narrative of kingship and worship.

King Solomon, renowned for his wisdom and ambitious architectural projects, sought to construct a temple of unparalleled splendor in Jerusalem. To achieve this, he forged critical alliances with the Sidonians, who were esteemed far and wide as exceptional timber cutters. Solomon engaged with the Sidonians for strictly pragmatic and strategic reasons. Although his goal was to harness their resources for his divine venture, his interaction with the Sidonians had unintended spiritual ramifications that rumbled through Israel's religious landscape.

Solomon's political strategy included marital alliances with foreign nations, including with the Phoenicians. The biblical texts tell us his many wives hailed from diverse backgrounds, including Moab, Ammon, Edom, Sidon, and the lands of the Hittites. Though politically astute, these marriages gradually introduced and then normalized within Israel the worship of foreign deities like Astarte and Baal. In trying to please his foreign wives, Solomon constructed high places devoted to these gods, laying the groundwork for future religious strife and idolatry within the kingdom.

Life in a Culture of Death

The entangled political and religious influences Solomon entertained set the stage for King Ahab, whose reign came a century or more after Solomon's.[2] The interval between their respective tenures was marked by gradual but significant shifts in Israel's religious fidelity and political allegiances.[3] When Ahab married Jezebel, the daughter of Sidon's king, Israel's religious and political realignments intensified, producing a staggering effect on Israel's religious life. Jezebel was more fervently devoted to the Phoenician deity (Baal) than Solomon's Sidonian queen had been. Jezebel actively promoted Baal worship across Israel and, in her zeal, more aggressively pushed idolatry. This exacerbated the conflicts over worship Solomon had inadvertently initiated.

Solomon set precedents and established patterns of foreign influence and idolatrous practice that have challenged the spiritual and political integrity of Israel for generations. The story of Israel and Sidon, woven through marriages, temples, gods, and kings, reveals the intricate and often perilous interplay between power and faith in the history of the ancient Near East.

God Sent Elijah *Where?*

Of all the places to send Elijah when the brook dried up, God chose Sidon, Jezebel's place of origin.[4] You might find a certain irony or perhaps divine humor in this directive. But might there be a deeper significance to the choice? Obviously, we cannot ask Elijah for insight, but we can piece together clues from the text.

We know Elijah's journey from Cherith to Zarephath was similar to his trip to the brook. Both journeys involved physical movement but emphasized God's ability to provide from the most unexpected sources. The two journeys serve as testaments to His mastery over all circumstances, His willingness to care for His servants, and His transcending of conventional boundaries. The story encourages us to broaden our understanding and realize God's care surpasses the limits of our familiar terrains and touches arenas beyond our limited expectations and perceptions.

Elijah's journey to Zarephath is also a substantial reminder of the God of Abraham, Isaac, and Jacob, a reminder of just who is the Lord of all creation. As Isaiah said on God's behalf to Cyrus, the king of Persia, "I am the LORD, and there is no other; besides me there is no god. I arm you, though you do not know me, so that they may know, from the rising of the sun and from the west, that there is no one besides me; I am the LORD, and there is no other" (Isaiah 45:5–6).

From Cherith to Zarephath, Elijah's journey exposes a difficult aspect of Elijah's relationship with his own community and reveals God's undaunted favor toward His prophet. Despite his calling, Elijah was rejected by his own people—not only unrecognized but also cast aside by those to whom God sent him. God's ways of providing for Elijah, at Cherith and afterward at Zarephath, were unusual because He is God but also because His ways serve as counterpoint to the prevailing consciousness.

Clearly, God's sending of Elijah into Jezebel's stomping grounds was not random. This plan was purposeful in regard to mission, and it remains instructive for our sakes.

In the Presence of His Enemies

Ironically perhaps, Elijah's move did not send him to friendlier territory. For all intents and purposes, Elijah arrived in enemy territory, a place marked by the distinctive culture of death. But why was he among supposed enemies?

If we fast-forward through Israel's history to what Scripture calls "the fullness of time" (Galatians 4:4–7), we find Jesus in the synagogue at Nazareth, His hometown. There, He holds the scroll of Isaiah and declares the coming of "the year of the Lord's favor" (Luke 4:16–30). Presumably, this was not enemy

Life in a Culture of Death

territory for a Nazarene. And surely, His prophetic announcement was one of divine grace and liberation reminiscent of the jubilee. Yet His words were not met with joy or even acceptance. Instead, His hearers expressed skepticism and outright offense. The One who proclaimed favor was treated with unvarnished disfavor.

In His hometown, Jesus was not seen as the Anointed One sent by God. To His neighbors, He was the son of Joseph the carpenter. Jesus' face was familiar in His neighborhood, but His posture of prophetic authority offended the people, and they refused to acknowledge it. Their resistance was more than a personal slight but emblematic of a deeper, historical pattern that consistently afflicted Israel's ancient prophets. Jesus Himself pointed out that while miracles and messages of hope were accepted by foreigners, like the widow of Zarephath and Naaman the Syrian, they were often rejected by the very people to whom they were first sent (Luke 4:24–25).

This rejection by Jesus' own people confirms a sorrowful truth about human nature and divine mission. The prophets who bore the burden of the Lord and carried history-making, Spirit-inspired words were often met with hostility and disbelief by their own communities. It is in this light we need to view the mission of Elijah, who finds refuge and acceptance in an unlikely place, a foreign land from which Jezebel hailed and in the house of an unlikely ally—a widow who was not of the children of Israel and who seemed to have nothing to offer a hungry traveler.

The Baals Fail, Then and Now

It is ironic to me that a queen as powerful as Jezebel worshiped powerless gods. Jezebel learned to worship them under her father's tutelage, so her gods were not newcomers to the pantheon of Sidon's idols. Yet they failed Jezebel's own people in their time of dire need. The Baals could provide neither rain nor dew, two essentials easily withheld in the name of Elijah's God.

This failure brings to light a striking case of cognitive dissonance, the psychological conflict that results when an entire people group holds contradictory beliefs or values as their shared experience—a part of their collective consciousness. Continuing to bow down at altars to gods that are no gods is costly. To dig in their heels as a people and redouble their efforts in false worship that leads nowhere necessarily raises a painful and perhaps unspoken question: Why persist? Yet except perhaps for one widow, they seem unable to abandon their false beliefs.

This collective cognitive dissonance isn't a relic of ancient civilizations; it is a disturbing trend within contemporary culture and even within segments of today's church. As society increasingly embraces a sense of entitlement and strives for dominion over those who dissent, a troubling current is emerging within various streams in the church. That current flows from certain postmodern cultural beliefs mistakenly embraced as divine mandates.

Consider the way some contemporary Christian groups interpret what is widely called the dominion mandate from Genesis 1:26–28. This Scripture passage calls humanity to steward God's creation and is often misconstrued as a call to political dominionism. Such interpretations suggest that achieving political power is synonymous with ushering in God's kingdom. This distortion mirrors the ancient Israelites' struggles with idolatry and the temptation to conform divine commands to human desires.

In truth, the dominion that God entrusts to humanity is not about power but about stewardship and care in returning the creation to its intended harmony with its Creator. It is a mandate to serve, not dominate; to heal and reconcile, not to conquer and divide. As followers of Christ, we are called

Life in a Culture of Death

to embody His values, which often stand in stark contrast to the prevailing winds of cultural power and entitlement. As the church navigates society's choppy waters, our task is not to seize political power but to be a transformative presence of salt and light in a world that needs the true hope of the gospel. This involves rigorous self-examination to ensure our actions, beliefs, and missions align with the teachings of Jesus rather than with transient cultural doctrines.

As we consider the failures of Jezebel's gods, let us also examine our own allegiances. Are we serving the God of Abraham, Isaac, and Jacob or gods of our own making? Are we seeking the kingdom of God or kingdoms of our own design? These are the questions that must guide us forward as we seek to obey God's true dominion mandate in our broken world.

Progress and Remembering

The cherished "spirit of Elijah" is about remembering who we are and maintaining the ancient pathways to wholeness and well-being. The late Spanish philosopher George Santayana tells us, "Progress, far from consisting in change, depends on retentiveness."[5] Considering this statement from a spiritual perspective helps us to understand true progress does not arise from change for its own sake. Instead, it depends upon our ability to retain and remember the core truths that have been entrusted to us through Scripture (Jude 3). When change becomes an absolute, we risk losing our foundational bearings and leave ourselves no direction for improvement. As Santayana warns, we end up perpetuating an infantile state in what we see as our spiritual maturity.

Santayana also cautions, "Those who cannot remember the past are condemned to repeat it."[6] This admonition is crucial today. In our eagerness to engage with, transform, or even "reform" the culture, we seem to have forgotten the lessons of our scriptural heritage. We often make the Scriptures say what we want them to say, rather than trusting what they actually say. Like the ancient Israelites, who repeatedly turned from God to follow the cultural idols of their time, we court danger by forgetting the divine mandates to us as stewards and caretakers, not dominators, of creation.

In his reflection on old age, Santayana notes it can be "as forgetful as youth, and more incorrigible; it displays the same inattentiveness to conditions; its memory becomes self-repeating and degenerates into an instinctive reaction, like a bird's chirp."[7] Regardless of our age or stage in life, this metaphor serves as a warning. Whether we cling to outdated man-made traditions without understanding their basis or embrace modern ideologies without discernment, we risk reducing our faith to base, instinctual reactions rather than thoughtful responses to the cross-shaped journey we are on, from faith to faith and from glory to glory (Romans 1:17; 2 Corinthians 3:18).

These days, my prophetic burden lies in reconnecting with the ancient wisdom that has withstood the test of time. The popular mantra "recency is relevancy" is misleading and often false. It's not necessarily true that "newer" means "more relevant." Although technological advancements that relieve us from a certain amount of toil are helpful and efficient, "new revelations" must be examined. If they are said to come from the Spirit but do not align with the ancient tenets of our faith, they are suspect. As we navigate such claims, we must anchor ourselves in the timeless truths that have guided generations before us.

We hear often about "engaging with culture," and such engagement is important. The question from a scriptural perspective is in *how* we engage with culture. Our attempts to engage need to be founded on deep engagement with Scripture and with the Tradition (with a capital *T*). By these pillars, we can interpret the sacred text with both reverence and thoughtful

Life in a Culture of Death

reflection. We must resist being swayed by every new trend as fiercely as we resist accepting rigid, man-made traditions that fail to convey Christ's love and justice. We are called to be a people who remember correctly, firmly grasping what is good, true, and beautiful in our faith while boldly addressing the needs and challenges of our time.

Consider how esteemed museums rely on skilled teams of curators. These professionals ensure history is not only preserved but also understood and appreciated. Similarly, we need curators of our Tradition who understand our times and know what should be done because they value and honor and do not devalue our past. These stewards of faith connect the enduring wisdom of our Tradition with the pressing issues of today, ensuring our heritage informs our present and guides our future.

From a genuinely prophetic perspective, the primary focus within the Tradition of the church has not been the reformation of culture per se, but the reformation of the church itself. This essential understanding has been muted in our contemporary dialogues. Historically, the church has understood that genuine transformation begins within the community of believers. As we allow the Spirit to conform us more closely to the image of Christ through cruciformity (cross-shaped, self-sacrificial, self-emptying love), our lives will become beacons of His transformative power to the world.

Having this inward view of reform is critical because it aligns with the scriptural admonition to first remove the log from our own eye, so we can see clearly to remove the speck from our brother's eye (Matthew 7:5). This acknowledgment humbles us and reminds us that renewal within the church leads to a more authentic and effective witness to the broader society.

Today's trending shift is toward the belief that we are called to reform the culture directly, often by employing the methods and means of power and politics. This approach subtly leads us to adopt the very tactics and values that we are called to transform

Prophetic Integrity and the Elijah Legacy

through the gospel. Therefore, I believe we must be wary of this shift. Too easily, it undermines our calling to be a distinct, holy community exemplifying God's kingdom and draws us to become a movement that seeks to coerce or dominate others.

In adhering to our Tradition, let us recall the reformation of the church is an ongoing process of repentance, learning, and holy living that draws us closer to God and models His love and justice to the world. As we reform ourselves by aligning our lives more closely with the Scriptures and the life of Christ, we naturally become agents of transformation in the culture around us, not through force but through the compelling witness of our communal and individual lives.

The Latin phrase often used to describe the process of church reform is *ecclesia reformata, semper reformanda*, meaning "the church reformed, always reforming." This concept originated in the Reformed tradition, emphasizing the idea that the church must continually reexamine itself and strive for greater fidelity to the gospel. The challenge, however, even among the Magisterial Reformers, was that some sought to establish a problematic relationship between church and state, occasionally replicating the very entanglements they initially aimed to reform.

The true Spirit of Pentecost never seeks to utilize the kingdoms of this world for its own purposes. Unlike earthly powers that often aspire to dominance through coercion or political maneuvering, the Pentecost Spirit testifies to one King, Jesus Christ, who already reigns supreme and is bringing all things into subjection to His eternal purpose. This divine movement is ongoing, whether we are attuned to it or not. It invites us to align ourselves with the kingdom of God, which transcends earthly realms and operates from the inside out, through transformation rather than imposition. The Spirit thereby calls us not to conquer but to convert, not to dominate but to disciple, and to embody a kingdom that is not of this world but is powerfully present within it.

Life in a Culture of Death

Strangely enough, these ideas are being resisted in some contemporary circles. Yet they are essential to living in our true vocation to faithful stewardship in self-sacrificial love. This balanced approach will guide us in making decisions that honor our past and responsibly shape our future. May we be ever mindful of this as we continue to walk the path of faithfulness together.

Moving and the Heart of God

Elijah's movement across geographical, cultural, and spiritual boundaries underscores a far-reaching theme. God's message and mercies are not confined to any one group but are meant for all humanity. In Luke's gospel, Jesus makes this point in no uncertain terms:

> I [Jesus] say to you in truth, there were many widows in Israel in the days of Elijah, when the sky was shut up for three years and six months, when a great famine came over all the land, and yet Elijah was sent to none of them, but only to Zarephath, in the land of Sidon, to a woman who was a widow.
>
> Luke 4:25–26 LSB

For a prophet who challenged a powerful ruling family, being sent by God to hide out in the land ruled by that family's relatives is, at best, counterintuitive. By the time God directs Elijah to move on, the drought Elijah prophesied was already causing widespread hardship. One might imagine Elijah's description as an unusual figure, clothed in camel hair and looking like a cave-dweller, would be well known, having been circulated among Israel's neighbors. With such a notorious appearance, Elijah needed to be exceptionally adept at concealing his identity wherever the effects of the drought were felt.

However, we must consider many factors. A primary reason for placing Elijah in a potentially hazardous situation could be to deepen his trust and dependence on God. By navigating danger, Elijah's faith could be significantly strengthened, reinforcing his reliance on God's provision and protection, much as his isolation experience had done. Placing Elijah in Zarephath, in the midst of Baal worshipers, serves as a dramatic demonstration of God's power and sovereignty, not just to Elijah but to all who hear of these events. This assignment shows God can sustain His prophet even in the heart of enemy territory, a truth that directly challenges Baal's authority and supposed power.

By sending Elijah to a non-Israelite widow, God broadens Elijah's (and Israel's) understanding of who is included in His plans, emphasizing the idea God's mercy and provision are not limited to the Israelites but extended to all humanity. This prepares Elijah for a more inclusive view of God's kingdom, aligning with the biblical trajectory that culminates in the global scope of the gospel. Each act of obedience under duress and each experience of God's faithful deliverance served to prepare Elijah for future acts requiring even greater faith. His prophetic ministry later involved confronting false prophets and priests and calling down fire from heaven, tasks that demanded immense courage and trust in God.

Elijah's life was not his own but was directed by a higher divine purpose. God's orchestration of events to sustain Elijah through the widow of Zarephath is significant on many levels. The Hebrew name for Zarephath (צרפת, or *Tsarefat*) carries significant meaning. It comes from the root word צרף (*tsaraf*), meaning "to smelt" or "to refine."[8] Zarephath is a place imbued with symbolic weight, and it speaks quite accurately of Elijah's journey, the widow's suffering, and our own lives. Zarephath symbolizes purification and refinement. Just as metals are purified through fire, Zarephath speaks to us of places or seasons in which we undergo trials but emerge refined.

In the foreign land of Zarephath, the prophet finds himself tested and shaped. Likewise, the widow is refined through her

Life in a Culture of Death

faith and actions. Her ultimate willingness to obey Elijah's request and her subsequent transformation are testaments to God's refining work in her life. Zarephath represents a crucible where faith and obedience are put to the test and transformation occurs. Both Elijah and the widow are pressed to the limits of their faith to rely entirely on God's provision. Elijah must deal with the prospect of being fed by someone who is destitute. The widow must confront the prospect of using her last bit of flour and oil on the prophet's say-so.

Through their shared experience, Elijah and the widow are transformed. Their faith only deepens, and their reliance on God is strengthened. God's call for Elijah to move on had its desired effect!

A Place and Space of Hope

Zarephath, a place and space of refining, stands as a symbol of the sacred place and space of hope in the human condition. Even in the depths of our darkest seasons, there lies hidden in the refining process a promise of renewal and sustenance. When we cross thresholds into new, refining chapters of life, our "Zarephaths" remind us God is working through our hardships and preparing us for greater things. In these spaces and places, our faith is tested but also fortified. As a result, our necessary reliance on God becomes transformative.

God's purposes always include the testing and refining of our character. Being in Zarephath and already under threat tested Elijah's integrity, perseverance, and commitment to God's commands. The testing that refined Elijah's character also clarified and strengthened his calling and readiness for future challenges. Through these layered purposes, God's placement of Elijah in Zarephath certainly played a part in his physical survival and the continuation of his prophetic duties. But it also deepened his faith, demonstrated God's transcendent mercy and power, and set the stage for a broader understanding of God's universal care and sovereign purposes across all human divides.

The fact Elijah found refuge with a troubled widow in Zarephath without his presence being reported to the local authorities is a miracle all by itself! The ways in which divine protection, human discretion, and the cultural dynamics of the time were orchestrated in the providence of God bring countless questions to the human mind and remind us of the adage, "God moves in mysterious ways, His wonders to perform."

The story of Elijah and the struggling widow is a case study of God's wonders. Imagine Elijah, a man in a very vulnerable position, being matched by God with the most vulnerable member of ancient society—a destitute widow. Could the plot have been any thicker? Vulnerability and weakness are things we seek to avoid at all costs. Yet they are often paths to rising out of our fears and entering into radical hopes.

What God did in Zarephath leaves no question He has more wonders in mind that involve Elijah, including a showdown that will come "like a refiner's fire" (Malachi 3:2). But that would come later, after God's refining fire purifies the faith of a rejected prophet and an utterly marginalized widow.

Soul-Searching Questions

- Elijah's journey from Cherith to Zarephath says a great deal about life's transitions. Reflect on the spiritual practices, mindsets, and lessons that can help you navigate life's transitions with trust in God. How can you honor one chapter's ending while remaining open to the beginning chapter ahead?
- How have you cultivated patience and faith during uncertain, "in between" times? How have you found

Life in a Culture of Death

strength in God's past faithfulness as you stepped forward into new chapters? Where do you see potential for growth in these areas?

- What practices, spiritual disciplines, prayers, and Scriptures help you to grieve each ending, find closure, and prepare your heart for the next chapter? How do they help you when you feel stuck in uncertainty or impatience about the chapter ahead?

8

On the Threshold of Flourishing

As the LORD your God lives, I have nothing baked, only a handful of meal in a jar, and a little oil in a jug; I am now gathering a couple of sticks, so that I may go home and prepare it for myself and my son, that we may eat it, and die.

1 Kings 17:12

The place of refinement has a threshold—a "point of entering or beginning" that must be crossed.[1] Zarephath, steeped in the culture of death, represents the unlikely places of refinement in which God hides us and His provision for us. Consider again the definition of the Hebrew root word *tzaraf* that suggests the smelting process and the idea God's provision often comes through our most difficult circumstances. When Elijah and the widow were immersed in difficulty, God brought them together and worked His purposes in, between, and through them.

First Kings 17:10 says that "when [Elijah] came to the gate of the town, a widow was there gathering sticks." Elijah called out to her and asked her for some water. Then, "as she was going to bring it, he called to her and said, 'Bring me a morsel of bread in your hand'" (v. 11). After all, God had appointed her to feed Elijah. Unaware of the divine arrangement, she gave Elijah her bad news, saying, "As the LORD your God lives, I have nothing baked, only a handful of meal in a jar, and a little oil in a jug; I am now gathering a couple of sticks, so that I may go home and prepare it for myself and my son, that we may eat it, and die" (v. 12).

That was not what Elijah expected to hear, but it did not negate the threshold moment. There was more at stake than meeting the needs of the widow and her son. The entire situation was about to demonstrate God's sustaining grace and His ability to provide abundantly when scarcity is rampant. God appointed the widow as part of His larger purposes through Elijah, and He attended to her seemingly little world through Elijah's "let there be." This poor woman, who had been left without rights when her husband died, mattered to Yahweh. He addressed her dire present state and let her know she had a future to embrace.

The Encounter at the Gate

Let's take a closer look at some of the details from the narrative. The widow outside the gate crossed the threshold just as Elijah arrived on the scene. She had first exited the door of her house and then exited the gate to her city. Her exit can be seen as an exodus, a departure from her familiar existence and an entrance into a sustained form of provision she could never have imagined.

The widow ultimately crossed that threshold back into her city, where the culture of death loomed large. However, she arrived with the Miracle Man. As he was known to do, he spoke a word that was beyond himself and beyond what was humanly possible. Returning through that gate with Elijah marked her

On the Threshold of Flourishing

entry into an entirely new chapter of life for her household. Before the encounter was over, she and her household were supplied with enough provision to keep them fed "for many days" (v. 15).

Still, in the threshold moment, the heaviness in the widow's soul remained. Threshold moments often come with a sense of anxiety. As someone wisely said, "There is no crossing of a threshold in life at any season when there is an absence of anxiety." Like the place where the ravens served Elijah, this threshold moment was also a liminal space, an in-between stage that brought with it the weight of the unknown and of what might or might not come next.

When the widow first saw Elijah, she was on what seemed to be her final mission. With whatever strength she had left, she set out to gather a few sticks, after which she planned to bake a last meal for herself and her son, then face what seemed unavoidable—their deaths from starvation. It is no wonder anxiety gripped her heart as she stepped out of her home that day. The threshold she crossed was both physical and existential. Her steps out of the city gate were heavy with despair, fear, and resignation. She was preparing for a dismal end.

Consider the existential anxieties she might have experienced. Perhaps she questioned her worth, her role as a mother, her seeming abandonment by life, hope, and the gods of her people (Baal and Ashtaroth). How did she process the finality of her impending death? Each step outside her door and through the city gate symbolized a surrender to her fate, an acceptance of what seemed inevitable.

Little did she know Providence had already set in motion a better course. Picture the scene. As she crossed the threshold, there stood Elijah, a prophet with a history-making word. At that moment, her primal fears and existential angst were met with divine intervention. She found Elijah standing at the very place of her deepest anxiety—and he came with God's message! More than exiting a chapter of death; she stepped into a brand-new beginning.

After her initial encounter with Elijah, the widow reentered her home, not with the lingering shadow of death that had haunted her but with the promise of life and hope. Elijah's presence signified God's intervention and care, making the crossing of the threshold a transformative moment. The home in which death once loomed was about to become a place of promise and provision.

Elijah's simple request for a morsel of bread and a drink of water seems small. But it carried significant weight, especially considering the widow's dire situation. Based on what Elijah perceived as God's instruction, his request was a test of both faith and relationship. Asking a struggling and vulnerable widow for food and water must have been difficult, even for a prophet. Yet the request was necessary to determine whether the relationship was in fact ordained by God.

At a fundamental level, Elijah's symbiotic relationship with the widow illustrates a core truth at the heart of God's design for humanity. It is not good for humans to be alone.

Languishing and Flourishing

Relationships are essential for survival but also for thriving. In the contemporary context, Dr. Corey Keyes describes the spectrum that ranges from languishing to flourishing. The dynamics of languishing affect significant portions of the population and can be present at any point in the adult lifespan.[2] This finding underscores the importance of trust and interdependence in our relationships. Keyes's research on mental health confirms that languishing, marked by a sense of stagnation and emptiness that affects the sufferers' overall well-being, is widespread in the adult population.

The effects of languishing include a person's diminished functioning in daily life. On the mental health continuum, flourishing is an optimal state and is the opposite of languishing. Flourishing individuals experience positive emotions, purpose, engagement, and meaningful relationships. Flourishing involves thriving in personal and social life, embodying the highest levels of mental health and well-being,[3] and having supportive relationships and a sense of community.

The widow, preparing to bake her last meal with what remained of her flour and oil, epitomized the state of languishing. Her life was marked by scarcity and hopelessness as she anticipated death for herself and her son. Yet through her unanticipated encounter with Elijah and her subsequent act of faith, a miraculous provision transformed her dire circumstances. When Elijah asked for a morsel of bread, he perceived it as within her means to provide it. Though it was difficult for him to ask, he knew her willingness to fulfill his request could lead to unimaginable blessings.

This was important, because her self-talk and her reality reflected a belief system rooted in scarcity and hopelessness. Her words—"I have nothing . . . only a handful . . . a little . . . gathering a couple . . . going to die"—revealed her life script, and made her languishing plain to see. Her existing belief system of "nothing except" had perpetuated a scarcity mindset. Therefore, transformation required a fundamental shift in how she observed, interpreted, and made meaning of her reality.

Elijah's request was designed by God to break the spell of the culture of death that had gripped the widow's consciousness. Simply by saying, "Bring me a morsel," the prophet invited her to interrupt her patterns of perception and embrace a new reality. Her acceptance of his invitation was an act of defiance against the oppressive, ambient culture of death, and a radical step of faith toward the culture of flourishing in God's kingdom.

Fundamental Shifts of Perception

As the widow prepared to feed Elijah, she moved from the mindset of scarcity to one of trust and abundance. She thought she was scraping the bottom of the barrel, yet she was about to discover God's inexhaustible supply. Her act of trust led to her continued sustenance, mirroring the daily manna God provided for the Israelites in the wilderness. Like their manna, her jar would never be exhausted, just as God's faithfulness never fails.

From a pastoral perspective, this story speaks directly to our current context. Many today are caught in a culture of languishing, struggling to find hope and meaning. At times, we too are laden with anxiety and invited to cross unexpected but liberating thresholds. Feeling trapped in our liminal spaces, the unknown ignites our fears. But at these critical junctures, Providence arranges encounters like that between the widow and Elijah—not to doom us but to release a new beginning we did not previously perceive. Stepping out in faith, even in small ways, can lead to profound transformation and flourishing, as it did for the widow.

Consider the anxieties you face and consider this truth: The presence of anxiety does not mean the absence of divine care. In fact, it often signals you are on the cusp of a significant transformation. Both Elijah and the widow were in grave need of sustenance and were on the cusp of a miracle. They had both carried the weight of their respective burdens and suffering. The prophet was suffering for his people and their future; the widow suffered for her future and that of her son. All seemed to hang in the balance.

But specters from the past were also in play. The widow's past included repressed sin and shame she hinted at later when she wondered whether Elijah's presence was meant to bring judgment upon her. Amid all that, the indication came that grace was already at work in her life. Despite her burden, pain, and

On the Threshold of Flourishing

suffering, the widow willingly risked engaging with Elijah. She had good reason to draw back from him. Her life experiences had taught her to compartmentalize her pain, and now death seemed certain. Yet she responded to Elijah's request for bread, humiliating for him but pivotal for both of them.

Beset by his own feelings of shame and frustration, Elijah nevertheless asked boldly for a morsel of bread, a testament to his unwavering faith. The woman also seemed moved by something beyond herself. Amid all her pain and anxiety, she recognized Elijah as a man of God, and she expressed some knowledge of God, saying, "As the LORD your God lives" (1 Kings 17:12). She associated her visitor with his God, although Elijah had not revealed who he was. She perceived he was a servant of Yahweh, the God who lives. Somehow, she was engaged in deep listening within herself, pressing on her conscious awareness so that she hungered and thirsted to know the living God.

This, I believe, is an example of when "deep calls to deep" (Psalm 42:7). Psalm 42 is a psalm of lament that expresses a pilgrim's yearning for God. It is a psalm of the sons of Korah, who escort and protect David when he flees for his life from his son Absalom and the revolt Absalom initiated. The psalmist yearns for Jerusalem and the way things used to be. The distress and pain come out in a cry expressed in metaphor. A tornado at sea sucks up water from the depths and causes it to spout above the surface of the water toward the heavens. The sons of Korah liken the depths of the agitated sea to the depths of the distressed human spirit when assaulted by overwhelming angst. The setting at sea evokes a place where no firm footing is possible and the threat of drowning is always present.

The distraught widow has no firm footing, yet her cry is heard by the compassionate and merciful God of Israel, who sent Elijah to her, more for her sake than for his. God could have sustained Elijah anywhere, but this widow needed a breakthrough and a solid footing. She needed to know she still had a future. Somewhere deep in her lament, she heard God's promise. Might it have come as a thought from her spirit, a simple instruction that prepared her at some level for the help soon to arrive? Is it possible she heard deep within her that a man of God from Israel was coming so she could provide for him and in return receive provision? Had she perceived a nudge to obey a coming stranger?

Nothing in the text indicates such happenings, but the story illustrates how our hearts connect with the divine. Austin Farrer speaks of the "causal joint"[4]—a connection point where God's influence interacts with the natural world without overriding our human freedom. In this way, God's will and presence gently guide us toward His purposes by way of a deep connection that goes beyond mere words.

Ecclesiastes 3:11 says, "He has made everything beautiful in its time. He has also set eternity in their [human] heart" (LSB). This suggests a deep-seated desire for something enduring and divine within us, a way God draws us to commune with Him, bridging the finite and the infinite. This communion invites us to share in His eternal nature, elevating our conversations and interactions to the level of divine dialogue.

For the widow of Zarephath, this type of listening from the depths of her broken heart allowed a shift in her perceptions. This shift was possible because God heard her cries and never left Himself without a witness. Something within the widow's heart awakened to a reality greater than the bleak and hopeless world she saw before her eyes. Elijah was God's instrument appointed for her to recover her lost hope.

An Internal Posture

Does reading the account from 1 Kings 17 raise questions about how to be led by the Spirit as the widow was led? We can try to imagine the flow of thoughts that might have come to

On the Threshold of Flourishing

her heart, but we have no way of confirming them. Yet in our own experiences, thoughts sometimes leave impressions strong enough to get our attention. We can call them promptings or inklings that come from deep within our hearts, and we can recognize the ring of authority that makes them seem weightier than other thoughts.

Listening for such leadings isn't about trying to hear something specific but about being aware of the stream of thoughts that come as we cooperate with the Spirit within us. This awareness takes time and isn't a technique. It is a discipline and an internal posture that we cultivate, much like preparing soil to receive seed and bring forth fruit. We have to bear in mind that Elijah's God was not familiar to the widow, and she wasn't necessarily seeking Him. The prophet Isaiah talked about such situations when he spoke by the Spirit on God's behalf, saying, "I was ready to be sought out by those who did not ask, to be found by those who did not seek me" (Isaiah 65:1).

Learning how to listen as well as discern is a lifelong journey. There are no shortcuts to communion with the triune God. Even when it comes to stepping out in the obedience of faith, I submit it means stepping out without having all the answers. If you want all the answers *before* you walk in faith, you might as well forget about moving forward. At some point, faith is manifested in the decisions we make. The widow chose to respond favorably to Elijah. That was her step forward based on what she was already wrestling with internally. She made a decision. It proved to be an excellent one, and the rewards were staggering. After she "did as Elijah said . . . she as well as he and her household ate for many days. The jar of meal was not emptied, neither did the jug of oil fail, according to the word of the LORD that he spoke by Elijah" (1 Kings 17:15–16).

However minor they might seem to be, choices rooted in faith can lead to wholly unforeseen transformations within and around us. Amid even a culture of darkness and death, choices guided by faith can lead us toward significant and promising but previously unnoticed thresholds. Such stepping points lead us into that which we need and desire but believe we cannot have.

Like the widow of Zarephath, who languished under the weight of scarcity and impending death, we sometimes languish in places of seeming impossibility. May we discover as she did that the place of flourishing is but one small step away.

Soul-Searching Questions

- In your times of communion with the Lord, allow Him to reveal your current state in the various areas of your life. As He helps you to develop a comprehensive sense of where you are physically, emotionally, spiritually, and otherwise, consider some specific, actionable first steps you can take to improve your overall well-being.

- Prayerfully ponder God's provision for you, including individuals or resources that can provide guidance, encouragement, and accountability. This might include friends, family members, mentors, life coaches, or mental health professionals. How can you reach out to these people or utilize these resources to help you stay motivated and on track as you work toward a more flourishing life?

- In what areas of your life do you feel a lack of motivation, joy, or purpose? Ask the Lord how these areas have impacted your overall well-being, and listen for His guidance. Even the smallest practical and spiritual steps can move you toward flourishing. Consider setting small, achievable goals that align with your values and interests. What new habits or activities can you introduce to bring more positive emotions, engagement, and meaning into your daily life?

9

Rising out of Dead Things

[Elijah] cried out to the LORD, "O LORD my God, have you brought calamity even upon the widow with whom I am staying, by killing her son?" Then he stretched himself upon the child three times, and cried out to the LORD, "O LORD my God, let this child's life come into him again."

1 Kings 17:20–21

The widow of Zarephath's story of hidden pain is deeply rooted in the cultural and religious context of her time and region. She was raised in the honor-shame paradigm that is characteristic of many ancient Near Eastern societies. The cultural emphasis is to maintain honor and avoid shame, and doing both is essential to an individual's social standing and relationships within the community.

In honor-shame cultures, the community's perception of an individual's actions is paramount. "Honor is a public claim to worth or value" that requires "public acknowledgment." Conversely, shame is the loss of honor and is often associated with public disgrace. These values are "external controls on behavior," motivating people to act in ways that will maintain or enhance their honor in the eyes of others and avoid actions that could bring shame upon themselves or their families.[1]

Because Sidon was an upper-class Phoenician city, the widow would have been acutely aware of the cultural dynamics affecting her standing in the community. Even if she enjoyed a prominent position while her husband was alive, his death turned her life upside down. Widows like her were particularly vulnerable. They often faced significant social and economic challenges and certainly lacked the protection their husbands once provided. In fact, the Hebrew term for widow, *almana*,[2] connotes a woman who has lost her male protector, is left without financial means, and is in need of special legal protection.[3]

This was the plight of the widow of Zarephath, who found herself at risk of being exploited and marginalized.[4] Her interaction with Elijah points to her precarious state. When he first asked her for bread, her sense of resignation made it clear she and her son were on the brink of starvation. Nevertheless, she was willing to share the last of their provisions with Elijah. This was largely an act of hospitality, a prized virtue that brought honor to hosts and demonstrated their loyalty to the community and its values.

As a settler or sojourner back in Tishbe, Elijah understood the plight of outsiders and empathized with the woman's delicate position. He hadn't been part of Tishbe's family-based social structure, and he lacked the support it offered. In his own way, he had been vulnerable, and like the widow, he learned to navigate his precarious circumstances with faith and resilience.[5]

Exposed to Scandal

We know from 1 Kings 17:19 that the widow took Elijah into her home. When he first arrived, she was a Phoenician worshiper

Rising out of Dead Things

of Baal and Ashtaroth. But after their initial encounter she embraced the God of Elijah and showed her lodger—the man of God—radical hospitality. Receiving Elijah into her home for an extended season was radical from a cultural perspective because it raised questions of sexual impropriety.[6] Ancient Near Eastern social norms and boundaries were strictly maintained, especially regarding interactions between men and women who were not related; therefore, her actions would have been unusual and potentially suspect.[7]

Strict social codes governed the norms surrounding hospitality, and widows were particularly expected to obey them. Violations would only invite misunderstandings within the community and increase the widow's vulnerability.[8] She knew a woman's honor was closely tied to her sexual propriety. She understood that any hint of an improper relationship could have severe social consequences. Yet she risked extending hospitality to the man of God. This underscored her desperate situation and her faith in Elijah's God, who had already demonstrated His provision and care to her household.

Suspicions of scandal in innocent situations are not unusual in Scripture. The gospel records false accusations that circulated because of the virgin birth. Even Joseph had to be convinced by God that Mary was a virgin who conceived by divine rather than human means (Matthew 1:18–25). God allowed Mary, the widow of Zarephath, and other servants of His to be misunderstood by their communities, knowing their journeys of faith ultimately reveal deeper truths about His nature and character.

For example, the widow's situation teaches us about the power of radical trust and the willingness to step out in faith regardless of the social ramifications. As is true of Mary's experiences as Jesus' mother, the widow's story also reveals God is not confined by human expectations or societal norms. He operates beyond the boundaries of our understanding, inviting us to listen deeply, discern His voice, and step forward in faith. The challenges and risks these women faced were not indicators of God's absence; they were opportunities for His glory to be revealed in surprising and profound ways.

The same applies to Elijah, who was now a sojourner in Zarephath and found himself vulnerable once again.[9] As a man not grounded in the established social structure, his presence in the widow's home could easily be viewed with suspicion.[10] His presence, divinely ordered to help both him and the widow, made both more susceptible to disrepute. They had no recourse but to navigate the complexities of their unusual situation, relying on God's provision as well as His protection.

By understanding the cultural context and the risks they took, we gain a greater appreciation for their courage and faith. Their actions challenge us to consider how we respond to divine calls that push us beyond our comfort zones and social boundaries. They also invite us to reflect on our own vulnerabilities and the ways God works through unlikely and risky situations to bring about His purposes. Our steps of faith, even when misunderstood, can become conduits for God's miraculous interventions, transforming our vulnerabilities into testimonies of His grace and power.

Retributive Justice

The story of the Sidonian widow and her son did not end with the miracle of provision that rescued them from death's door. It continued with a second crisis—the actual death of the widow's son and the accusation her grief triggered.

> After [the miraculous provision of the meal and oil] the son of the woman, the mistress of the house, became ill; his illness was so severe that there was no breath left in him. She then said to Elijah, "What have you against me, O man of God? You have

Rising out of Dead Things

come to me to bring my sin to remembrance, and to cause the death of my son!"

1 Kings 17:17–18

The shock of her son's death raised painful issues for the widow, leading her to accuse Elijah of coming to Zarephath to address her sin. Her reaction reveals the degree to which she had internalized the honor-shame dynamic. As a widowed mother, her remaining hope for the future relied upon her child's well-being. Therefore, her son's death implied more than a shocking loss. The tragedy threatened to obliterate whatever societal standing she still had and jeopardize her means of survival. In essence, the death of her son was the death of her future.

In addition, the widow perceived her son's passing as a divine judgment. This way of interpreting tragic events is common in honor-shame cultures that tend to view misfortune as the result of personal or communal sin. This perspective underscores the deep connections by which one's actions are linked to the community's perceptions and to the favor or disfavor of the gods.[11]

This dynamic was seen as retributive justice, the idea of a balance by which one's punishment for sin is proportional to the offense. Such justice is based on the principle of an eye for an eye and is deeply rooted in the belief that moral order is maintained by ensuring wrongdoers receive their just deserts.[12] The widow's belief that she had fallen victim to retributive justice only deepened her despair and sense of loss. She concluded Elijah's presence brought her sin to light and caused her son's death—a deduction consistent with the belief that calamities are divine punishments for hidden sins. Her fear of retribution preceded her son's death and had long been brooding below the surface of her conscious awareness. Her experience reminds us to be vigilant, realizing the powers of darkness exploit such beliefs to inflict guilt and shame and potentially produce a shame-based identity.

The widow's accusation against Elijah shows she fully believed in retributive justice. Therefore, she could only interpret her son's death one way—as divine punishment for her sins. In her mind, she hadn't only lost her son; she was responsible for his death. This belief system was grounded in the notion the gods were actively involved in the lives of humans, dispensing rewards to those whose deeds were righteous and penalties to those who transgressed. Because all have sinned, the threat of retribution hung over every life as a way of making sense of suffering and maintaining a moral and social order within the community.

Shame and Blame

The widow's grief was raw—so raw it triggered accusation against Elijah. In a split second of time, her internalized guilt and shame coalesced with the cultural conditioning deep within her psyche, and before she even had a chance to think about what she was saying, she laid blame on Yahweh's prophet, making him her scapegoat.

Psychologically, scapegoating occurs when an individual or group unfairly blames others for their problems or misfortunes, "redirecting negative feelings and frustrations onto a safer target rather than addressing the actual source of the problem."[13] Projection provides temporary respite from deep feelings of guilt, shame, or inadequacy and allows individuals to transfer the emotional burden to someone else. But it only intensifies and further embeds the first person's shame-based identity, precisely what the demonic intends. The widow of Zarephath used the projection of blame as a defense mechanism by which she unloaded or externalized her own guilt and fear to alleviate the "anxiety that arises from psychic conflict."[14]

From a spiritual perspective, the projection of blame can be understood as a tactic of spiritual warfare. In Revelation 12:10, Satan is referred to as "the accuser of our brethren"

Rising out of Dead Things

(NKJV), highlighting his way of sowing seeds of doubt, guilt, and condemnation among believers. The widow's reaction can be seen as a manifestation of Satan's influence. Yet he first exploited her grief and vulnerability to turn her against Elijah and by extension against God. We need to be vigilant, understanding this satanic strategy—to exploit feelings of guilt by first inflicting shame and fear on the suffering soul and then tempting that person to retaliate by accusing others and causing them to experience the same pain.

The widow's crisis is a poignant example of how spiritual warfare can operate through our deepest fears and insecurities. The adversary seeks to amplify our feelings of guilt and unworthiness, leading us to blame others and doubt God's goodness. Recognizing this strategy helps us understand the importance of guarding our hearts and minds, turning to God in prayer, and relying on His truth to dispel the lies of the Enemy.

Shame Resilience

In the ancient world, it was unlikely anyone helped the suffering widow consciously understand her shame or build resilience to counteract its toxic effects. Today we can access such benefits, however. Researcher and author Brené Brown defines *shame* as "the intensely painful feeling or experience of believing that we are flawed and therefore unworthy of love, belonging, and connection."[15] She has also developed what she calls "shame resilience theory" (SRT) to help us better understand and address the issue.

Shame resilience involves recognizing and addressing shame in a way that promotes healing, connection, and personal growth. Brown describes four key elements of her theory:[16]

1. "Recognizing shame and understanding its triggers." This involves identifying the physical and emotional

signs of shame so we can become more aware of when shame is in play.

2. "Practicing critical awareness." This means understanding the societal and cultural expectations that contribute to feelings of shame so we can demystify and contextualize our shame experiences and reduce their power.
3. "Reaching out." This involves forming empathetic relationships and seeking support from others who can offer understanding and compassion.
4. "Speaking shame." Openly talking about our shame diminishes its power, making it possible to break the silence and secrecy that often surround shame. This helps us to foster a sense of control and resilience.

Because shame is an enduring feature of our fallen world, becoming more consciously aware of it helps us to develop the shame resilience that leads to greater emotional openness and increasing freedom from shame's grip.

Remember that for the widow of Zarephath, the culture's patriarchy and disregard for her needs and dignity immersed her in shame. She became isolated "on the fringes of society,"[17] with little hope of respite from her low estate. To whom could she reach out and break her silence? How could she reverse her vulnerability and diminish shame's power?

Under the circumstances, the widow was powerless to break free. But Yahweh stepped into the gap as the advocate and protector that society had denied her.[18] In her divine encounter with God through His servant Elijah, resilience became a journey not only of self-awareness but of God's presence drawing near to transform her pain into peace.

I believe Brown's framework finds its richest expression in the God who bears our burdens and upholds our worth. To the

Rising out of Dead Things

emotional path of shame resilience He adds a vital, spiritual passageway. His heart is to restore us amid our isolation, heal our wounds, and remind us that we are never alone. In His compassion, God makes a way for us to move beyond shame into a life awash in His care and ceaseless love.

Repression and Suppression

To better grasp the widow's struggle, we need to understand the concepts of repression and suppression. Repression is an unconscious process by which we keep distressing thoughts, memories, or desires out of our conscious awareness.[19] It is as though the mind protects itself by burying these painful elements deep enough within us to make us unaware of their existence, at least at a conscious level. Yet their "burial" does not keep them from influencing our behavior and emotions in powerful and often negative ways.

Suppression is a bit different. It is a deliberate choice to avoid thinking about certain troubling aspects of our lives.[20] Unlike repression, suppression requires a conscious effort to push distressing thoughts or feelings out of our awareness. Each function works in its own way to avoid and compartmentalize that which seems too painful to ponder.

The widow's lament is a window into her repressed and suppressed guilt. The former lies buried in her unconscious mind and surfaces indirectly through her actions and feelings. The latter is also pushed aside, but at a conscious level and with lingering effects. Her example helps us to understand both issues so we can recognize our own unresolved guilt and shame, as well as understand how they shape our behaviors and emotions in ways we might not immediately perceive.

If we understand the signs, we become cognizant of our own patterns of repression and suppression. In a broad sense, repression can manifest as unexplained anxieties, recurring negative patterns, or emotional responses that seem disproportionate to the situation. Suppression can show up as a persistent effort to distract ourselves from painful thoughts or feelings by keeping our attention focused elsewhere. Both approaches are essentially diversions that undermine our psychological health, hinder our spiritual growth, and compromise our well-being.

We cannot afford to ignore or dismiss the fact the powers of darkness are always lurking in the background of our lives and impacting the shadowy places in our hearts. Their intent is to exploit our guilt and shame, just as they exploited the widow's. These powers of darkness execute their methods with torment, because "fear involves torment" (1 John 4:18 NKJV), the demonic's stock-in-trade.

Perfect Love as Antidote

There is only one antidote to torment—the "perfect love" of God that is complete, mature, and selfless (v. 18). This love is fully realized and expressed, leaving no room for the fear associated with punishment and judgment. When we are perfected in God's love, we become confident in our relationship with Him, knowing His love is without conditions or end. His love is not only for the whole world but for us as individuals.

God's perfect love is unconditional because it is not based on our actions or worthiness to receive it. It is selfless because God always seeks the best for His beloved (vv. 16–18). Perfect love is also complete and mature. The Greek word *teleia*, translated "perfect" in 1 John 4:18, expresses both of these qualities.[21] God's love is fully developed and rooted in the assurance of His grace and mercy. Therefore, His love casts out the fear that comes from the anticipation of punishment. The fear of condemnation leaves when we know we are accepted and loved by God (Romans 8:38–39).

Rising out of Dead Things

In Psalm 139, David closes with a powerful prayer to God. "Search me, O God, and know my heart; test me and know my thoughts. See if there is any wicked way in me, and lead me in the way everlasting" (Psalm 139:23–24). We can pray this simple prayer, asking the Holy Spirit to search our hearts and reveal any ways in which we might be repressing or suppressing aspects of our inner selves. This is what David did, and when we do it we invite the Spirit to shine His light into the deepest recesses of our souls and expose any hidden fears, anxieties, or painful thoughts we might have consciously or unconsciously buried there. This prayer opens us to God's transforming grace and allows Him to heal any hidden wounds, recurring patterns, disproportionate emotional responses, or unexplained anxieties. He can free us from the bondage of repression and suppression, so we can experience true spiritual growth, well-being, and the abundant life Christ has promised us.

Death Is Not the Final Answer

When the widow's son died, she entered a state of excruciating grief and deep confusion. As she grappled with her loss, the fear of divine judgment, and her inner sense of unworthiness, she blamed her son's death on the prophet whom God sent to save her family. Her reaction reminds us of the power of guilt and shame to distort our perception of God's work in our lives. The woman who previously saw Elijah as a man of God temporarily lost perspective and saw him as an instrument of judgment.

Thankfully, Elijah did not respond in kind. He simply said, "Give me your son." Then "he took him from [the widow's] bosom, carried him up into the upper chamber where he was lodging, and laid him on his own bed" (1 Kings 17:19). Elijah did not lash out or defend himself. He took the widow's pain seriously and brought it before God, even placing the blame on God by saying, "O Lord my God, have you brought calamity even upon the widow with whom I am staying, by killing her son?" (v. 20).

Elijah's reaction reveals his own struggle to understand God's ways, and it shows that some aspects of his faith were still being perfected. But the narrative takes a transformative turn when Elijah is moved by compassion, performs a prophetic act, and prays fervently to God. The text says "he stretched himself upon the child three times, and cried out to the Lord, 'O Lord my God, let this child's life come into him again'" (v. 21).

Let's note certain details within the narrative. In verse 19 of the passage, Elijah picked up the child and ascended to his own "upper room" in the widow's house. This place of rest and retreat was now a liminal space between heaven and earth. Their ascent echoes the imagery of Jacob's ladder, the gate of God, and the house of God (Genesis 28:12, 17)—a place where the divine and human realms intersect.

In this sacred space, Elijah embraced the dead child. This was an act of deep compassion and identification with human mortality. He stretched himself upon the boy, not once but three times. This symbolic deed resonates with the scriptural significance of the number three, which expresses divine completeness, wholeness, and the intensity of God's presence (Genesis 18:2; Jonah 1:17; Matthew 26:34–35). Elijah's stretching himself upon the child powerfully foreshadowed Christ's stretching on the cross, where He fully identified with our human brokenness and mortality in order to conquer death and raise us to new life. Just as Elijah stretched himself three times, Christ endured the full weight of human suffering, descending into the depths of death itself, only to rise victorious on the third day.

When Elijah prayed for the boy to be restored to life, "the Lord listened to the voice of Elijah." After the third stretching, "the life of the child came into him again, and he revived" (1 Kings 17:22). This miracle can only be understood in light of the incarnation, by which the eternal Word became flesh.

Christ did not merely enter into time; He transformed time, effecting redemption from the beginning to the end. The metaphysical dimension of the incarnation is woven into the fabric of this miracle. The ancient voices of Irenaeus of Lyons and Athanasius of Alexandria both proclaim: "He became what we are so that we might become what He is."[22] Indeed, it is Christ who "brought life and immortality to light through the gospel" (2 Timothy 1:10).

Once the boy was revived, Elijah brought him down from the upper room, "gave him to his mother . . . [and] said, 'See, your son is alive'" (1 Kings 17:23). This was a symbolic re-entry into earthly existence from the place where death had been conquered. Their descent from Elijah's chamber mirrors Christ's own descent from the heavenly realms, bringing the gift of eternal life to a world trapped in the shadow of death.

The reviving of the widow's son was an act of divine intervention and a glorious demonstration of the perfect love that transcends human guilt and shame and offers grace and restoration instead of punishment. This story is a powerful reminder that with God, even death is not the final answer.

Religion, Pure and Undefiled

Elijah's journey with the widow and her son in 1 Kings 17:17–24 is rich with insights into the spiritual disciplines of listening deeply, discerning wisely, and stepping forward in faith. Throughout Elijah's stay with the widow of Zarephath, he was open, trusting, vulnerable, and transparent. There was almost a hint of tenderness about him, a seeming anomaly for the often aloof and fiery figure.

It may be that Elijah's usual temperament stemmed from his ascetic manner of listening deeply to the Lord. Perhaps, however, his personality and history as a sojourner formed his self-consciousness as a solitary figure. In any case, his time with the widow seemed to stretch Elijah inwardly far more than he stretched his physical frame over the dead boy's body. It appears God used a Gentile widow to expand Elijah's relational capacity, even as she unjustly blamed him for her son's death. Elijah's responses reveal his humanness, tenderness, love, and concern for her. If faith works by love (Galatians 5:6), the faith needed to raise the widow's son from death may have worked through the love Elijah developed for her, a woman burdened with a debilitating sense of shame, blame, and hopelessness.

Surely, raising her child from the dead wasn't an act of Elijah's will or a determination to perform a miracle. The child's death, the widow's plight, and the prophet's vulnerability all contributed to a kind of relational chemistry that changed them for the better. The apostle James, who speaks of Elijah in the last chapter of his letter to the saints, says something in the first chapter that might also reference the fiery prophet of old. "Religion that is pure and undefiled before God, the Father, is this: to care for orphans and widows in their distress, and to keep oneself unstained by the world" (James 1:27).

By speaking of religion that is "pure and undefiled," James implies religion can be impure and defiled. Elijah's actions toward the widow of Zarephath and her son exemplify the pure and undefiled religion James described. Genuine worship, or *thrēskeía*,[23] involves more than external rituals; it encompasses the reverence, godliness, and devotion that arise from a reverent fear and an acceptance of God's direction. Elijah practiced both by caring for the distressed widow and praying fervently for her son's life to be restored. The prophet's compassionate response and faith-filled actions exemplify the heart of true worship. His ministry is a powerful reminder that tangible acts of pure and undefiled mercy and love reflect the very character and purposes of God.

If these qualities are aspects of what we call the spirit of Elijah, may we listen deeply to the One who calls us to the same. May we also discern clearly how we are to act, and then step

Rising out of Dead Things

out in faith and allow Him to express His love and life through us in every situation. In this way, we can rise out of dead things, participate faithfully in the ongoing work of God's kingdom, and carry hope and healing to a world in need.

Soul-Searching Questions

- Consider your experiences with shame in its different forms. In what ways has a shame-based identity made you feel unworthy or hindered your ability to move forward in personal relationships, career, or self-growth? What steps can you take to separate your identity from these feelings of shame, and who can support you in this journey toward healing and self-acceptance?
- How can you differentiate between the healthy shame that leads to positive changes and the toxic shame that serves only as self-punishment? Reflect on a recent situation in which you felt ashamed. Did the feeling motivate you to correct a specific behavior (healthy shame), or did it lead to self-condemnation and a sense of unworthiness (toxic shame)? How can recognizing this difference help you to respond more constructively to feelings of shame?
- What are some of the negative self-beliefs or internalized messages that contribute to your experience of toxic shame? Consider the origins of these beliefs—whether from childhood experiences, societal pressures, or past traumas. How can you begin to challenge and reframe these beliefs to cultivate self-compassion and reduce the impact of toxic shame on your mental and emotional well-being?

10

The Hour Has Come

After many days the word of the LORD came to Elijah, in the third year of the drought, saying, "Go, present yourself to Ahab; I will send rain on the earth."

1 Kings 18:1

"Many days" after God restored the widow's son to life, God called His servant Elijah to another face-off with Ahab. This confrontation would be more than a clash between the prophet and the wicked king; it would be the collision of opposing worldviews.

Elijah's worldview was centered in the God of Abraham, Isaac, and Jacob, who revealed His name, YHWH, to Moses at the burning bush. This name, known as the tetragrammaton, is composed of four Hebrew letters: Yod, He, Vav, He. As the most sacred and revered name of God in the Hebrew tradition, YHWH reveals the very essence of God and signifies His eternal, unchanging, and ever-present nature. It also encapsulates the intimate and covenantal relationship between God and His people. The name is so sacred that, even today,

YHWH is seldom spoken aloud in the Jewish tradition, and other titles (such as *Adonai* for "Lord") are used in its place. Understanding the sacredness of YHWH helps us to grasp the full weight of Elijah's confrontation with Ahab. When he confronted the forces of Baalism, Elijah did not act in his own name or power. He wielded the authority and power of YHWH as he invoked the sacred name, embodied YHWH's divine presence, and asserted the supremacy and sovereignty of the one true God. The battle royale between Yahwism and Baalism had come to a head, with Elijah on one side and Ahab on the other.

Out of Hiding and into the Fray

As is true of Elijah's entire tenure as a prophet of God, the 1 Kings 18 narrative includes lessons about listening and discerning. The chapter begins with the words "After many days," indicating a significant period of time has elapsed since Elijah had prayed for the life of the widow's son to be restored.

We have seen that up to this point, Elijah had received divine guidance regarding provision and survival, for himself and the widow of Zarephath. Now, however, God was sending him to present himself to Ahab and tell him the Lord "will send rain on the earth" (v. 1). "So Elijah went to present himself to Ahab" (v. 2).

Of course, this was a dangerous mission. Delivering the message that appeared to be good news nevertheless drew Elijah out of hiding and exposed him to the powers that sought to silence and even annihilate him. The message about the return of rain had been a long time coming, and Israel had sustained much damage since the drought began. Ahab and Jezebel would surely hold Elijah responsible for that. He had managed to elude them for more than three years, but now he was forced out of obscurity and into the open. There, the powers that motivated Ahab and Jezebel and sought to kill Elijah could more easily accomplish their aim.

The Hour Has Come

Clearly, Elijah was positioned for a dramatic confrontation with the malevolent powers that had poisoned Israel. Ever since Elijah first prophesied the drought, God's dealings with Him pointed to this pivotal moment. His period of extended absence served God's purposes, but questions had almost certainly been raised during that time about where Elijah was and when he might resurface. Now those questions will be answered, and Elijah and Ahab will come face-to-face.

Bear in mind, however, that the king's standing was not what it had been. The drought had long since sullied his reputation, along with the reputation of the gods he and Jezebel endorsed. These false deities had failed miserably, having been proven entirely unable to provide even a drop of rain over the course of forty-two months. Needless to say, there was plenty of bad press to go around for those earthly and otherworldly beings who lorded over Israel's suffering people! Their failures did not surprise Elijah. They only served to validate Elijah's poor opinion of Baal and his recognition of the king's utter disdain for those under his rule.

For all these reasons, Ahab had good reason to fear Elijah's reappearance—and reappear he would.

Friends in High Places

Meanwhile, Ahab scrambled to deal with the lingering drought and severe famine. He "summoned Obadiah, who was in charge of the palace," and ordered him to find any remaining patches of grass that might help sustain the king's horses and mules destined to otherwise perish (1 Kings 18:3, 5). Although Obadiah served in the king's court, he "revered the LORD greatly" (v. 3). While Jezebel was "killing off" God's prophets, Obadiah managed to save one hundred of them by hiding them in two caves and providing bread and water for their sustenance (v. 4). Given the severity of the famine and his position in the court, Obadiah's surreptitious care of God's servants required a great logistical effort. By caring for the prophets, Obadiah ensured Jezebel's failure in her goal to wipe out Yahweh's servants altogether.

However, still duty bound as a member of Ahab's court, Obadiah searched for the grassy places the king desperately needed. On the way, he unexpectedly crossed Elijah's path. "Obadiah recognized him, fell on his face, and said, 'Is it you, my lord Elijah?' He answered him, 'It is I. Go, tell your lord that Elijah is here'" (vv. 7–8).[1]

The presumed chance meeting between Obadiah and Elijah was consequential and potentially fatal for Obadiah, whose prominent position carried immense responsibility and required a high level of trust. Obadiah's high profile also kept him under Jezebel's watchful eye. As manager of the king's household, Obadiah oversaw domestic affairs and influenced political matters. Therefore, his loyalty and reliability were paramount. The king had to entrust him with access to members of the royal family and to sensitive information and resources.

Obadiah understood the delicacy of his situation and Elijah's. When Elijah told him to summon Ahab, Obadiah was shaken and asked, "How have I sinned, that you would hand your servant over to Ahab, to kill me? As the Lord your God lives, there is no nation or kingdom to which my lord has not sent to seek you" (vv. 9–10). Obadiah knew carrying Elijah's message to the king would almost certainly mean his own ruination. So he pleaded with Elijah:

> You say, "Go, tell your lord that Elijah is here." As soon as I have gone from you, the spirit of the Lord will carry you I know not where; so, when I come and tell Ahab and he cannot find you, he will kill me, although I your servant have revered the Lord from my youth. Has it not been told my lord what I did when Jezebel killed the prophets of the Lord, how I hid a hundred of the Lord's prophets fifty to a cave, and provided them with bread and water? Yet now you say, "Go, tell your lord that Elijah is here"; he will surely kill me.
>
> 1 Kings 18:11–14

The Hour Has Come

Undeterred, Elijah answered, "As the LORD of hosts lives, before whom I stand, I will surely show myself to him today" (v. 15). Elijah entreated Obadiah to confront his fears, responsibilities, and the authenticity of his faith. He also reassured the shaken man, saying, "As the LORD of hosts lives . . . I will surely show myself to [Ahab] today." By invoking the sacred name, Elijah helped to ground Obadiah in a hopeful reality. There was no higher form of assurance Elijah could offer than to remind Obadiah of the God who cannot lie. Thus, meeting up with Elijah proved empowering and enabled Obadiah to transcend his existential dread and fulfill his duty. Obadiah "went to meet Ahab, and told him [what Elijah said], and Ahab went to meet Elijah" (v. 16).

This outcome was another act of defiance and courage that spoke volumes about Obadiah's character and deep reverence for God. The text gives no hint as to how Obadiah accomplished all he did while working for the reprobate royal couple. We can only infer that as the drought progressed, sustaining the palace and the hidden prophets required great ingenuity, wisdom, and determination on Obadiah's part.

Obviously, both Obadiah and Elijah served God knowing they could be executed as traitors. While Obadiah served from within the court's inner circle, Elijah was a voice crying out in the wilderness. Although Elijah was unbound by the constraints of the palace, his prophetic mission was to speak truth to power. Therefore, he would have to confront Ahab and Jezebel directly by challenging their idolatry and leading the people back to the worship of Yahweh. Executing his mission demanded he come into close contact with his adversaries.

Though their assignments were unique, both Elijah and Obadiah were exactly where God intended them to be. Obadiah's quiet, behind-the-scenes faithfulness proved as crucial as Elijah's dramatic public engagement. Obadiah worked within the system, using his position to protect God's prophets and maintain a remnant of faith within a corrupt regime. Elijah operated outside the system, boldly proclaiming God's message and calling for national repentance.

This juxtaposition reminds us God's purposes are fulfilled through diverse forms of service. Our own callings may or may not be dramatic or public. More often than not, our callings involve quiet faithfulness in challenging circumstances. Either way, God works in us and through us.

Fear and Anxiety in a Very Real Crisis

Imagine yourself standing at the edge of a dense forest, with the path ahead shrouded in mist. You know there's a beautiful meadow ahead, but the sound of rustling leaves and distant feral howls makes you wary. Notice how this imaginary scenario mirrors a common human experience—the tendency to focus on immediate dangers rather than trusting in God's broader, overarching plan.

Now put yourself in Obadiah's shoes as he unexpectedly crossed Elijah's path and considered his predicament from a personal perspective. The drought had been underway for more than three years and had now reached a point where even the cattle and livestock were dying. As if that weren't stressful enough, picture yourself hiding and feeding one hundred prophets of Yahweh— under the very nose of the queen who wants to slaughter every last one of them.

Would you experience anxiety in such a scenario? I would! Anyone in Obadiah's shoes would have to keep one eye over their shoulder, expecting the sword of Damocles to fall. Nobody knew this better than Obadiah. Under the best of circumstances, his job as a palace administrator was thankless. He had the added misfortune of serving under a king and queen who were anything but honorable, and he knew exactly what they were capable of doing. Yet he also knew he had to preserve what was left of the prophetic community Jezebel was working to eradicate.

The Hour Has Come

With every surreptitious act Obadiah performed—with every word he spoke and every step he took—he knew what hung in the balance, not only his life but the lives of one hundred prophets who faced grave danger if Obadiah was found out. Perhaps there is no rest for the wicked, but neither would there be any rest for righteous Obadiah.

Meeting up with Elijah only seemed to complicate Obadiah's already precarious situation. Obadiah knew who Elijah was and recognized him immediately. He knew Elijah had made some unexpected entrances and quick departures in the past, and he fully expected Elijah to repeat this pattern in the future. So when Elijah told Obadiah to notify the king he had returned, Obadiah had every reason to be fearful. His candid response to Elijah revealed his internal struggle. Three times, he mentioned Ahab would kill him (1 Kings 18:9, 12, 14). He openly confessed his fear and anxiety, justified and rooted in Jezebel's proven track record of vengeance against God's servants.

Psychoanalysts might argue that Obadiah's fear represented an unconscious fear of death. However, I believe his fear was fully conscious and active at this point in the narrative. Obadiah's "what if" thinking is characteristic of anxiety and centers on a worst-case scenario. He did not run from his fear; he owned it and advocated for himself. His transparent expression offers us valuable insight into the importance of acknowledging and addressing our anxieties during unfamiliar or challenging situations.

Obadiah had cause to be anxious. He wasn't only concerned with the immediate danger he faced; he also harbored fears of the unknown. He told Elijah, "As soon as I have gone from you, the spirit of the LORD will carry you I know not where" (v. 12). Elijah had been known to disappear, and Obadiah connected this behavior to God's way of operating in Elijah's life. He could only conclude that controlling or predicting Elijah's comings and goings would be impossible.

This realization only exacerbated Obadiah's anxiety and caused him to wonder whether Elijah realized all he had already risked. Obadiah also wondered whether he—a faithful servant of Yahweh—was utterly doomed, as Elijah's disappearance seemed inevitable, and Obadiah's own death would almost certainly result.

In pleading his case, Obadiah employed what psychologists call *rationalization*. Under the circumstances, this was a normal defense mechanism and not an aberrant response. In an attempt to mitigate his current fear and any potential judgment from Elijah and God, Obadiah simply emphasized his loyalty and the risks he had already taken.

Obadiah's identity was caught between his loyalty to God and his role in Ahab's court. These opposing demands created an unavoidable internal conflict that manifested in his dialogue with Elijah. Some psychologists might view this as an ego conflict in which Obadiah's sense of self was torn between opposing allegiances. I am not persuaded that is the case. There is no question Obadiah was loyal to Yahweh. There is also no question his responsibilities as palace administrator demanded his compliance. I believe the tension he experienced was inherent to the role God had prepared for him long before his current predicament manifested.

Obadiah's inner conflict probably had far more to do with his need for clarity as he walked the tightrope he was on. He intuitively knew every action he took was meaningful and consequential. He felt the great weight of responsibility to his God and his people, and by the grace of God he navigated all of it. If you have been in a position to make choices under threatening conditions, you know Obadiah's anxiety was warranted. If you haven't been in his shoes, you might pray you never have to wear them.

Either way, you can glean valuable insights from Obadiah's handling of a seemingly untenable position and his choice to brave existential danger. May we all resist the urge to judge those who bear such burdens as he bore. And may we pray for them as they honestly grapple with the dread that could easily overwhelm any mortal soul.

Authenticity in Elijah's Day

In contemporary culture, we hold the idea of authenticity in high regard. Everywhere we turn, we are encouraged to be ourselves, be vulnerable, live "our truth" openly, and express our individuality, thoughts, and feelings without pretense. This openness and transparency mean that what we feel inside and what we show to the world are necessarily consistent.

All these ideas are now staples of social media and other public discourse. They have even affected how we brand ourselves personally and professionally. But let's journey back to the ancient Near East, where authenticity involved honor, duty, loyalty, and a reverent fear of God. These were the very qualities Obadiah demonstrated as he walked the thin line so fraught with danger.

Obadiah's authenticity—his true self—emerged in his moments of fear, courage, and unwavering commitment to God and duty, most of which were hidden from public view. Elijah was also authentic. He stood boldly and publicly for God. He was ready to challenge Ahab and the prophets of Baal, and he was committed to calling the people back to Yahweh. His authenticity showed in his fearless proclamation not of "his truth" but of God's truth and his own unwavering mission. Even now, Elijah's life stands as a testament to faith and the role of the prophet.

We can learn so much about authenticity from Elijah, Obadiah, and the ancient Near Eastern culture, particularly from the standpoint of scriptural faithfulness to God and integrity in our roles in life. May we, like Obadiah, be courageous in our hidden acts of loyalty. And, like Elijah, may we be bold in our public witness. May our authenticity be rooted not in self but in our honor, duty, and reverence for the One who calls us. And let us remember that when we are weak, we are strong.

In fact, we learn to listen to the Spirit's leading not by fleeing from our weakness but by abiding in it and trusting in God's greater plan and the Spirit's empowering presence.

This is what Jesus taught us as He embraced the cross and all its consequences. He is not only the truth and the life. He is *the way*. If we listen deeply, we will discover Jesus Himself is the journey through all our dilemmas. In Him, we can overcome life's existential and psychological conflicts and make a significant impact on our generation.

Soul-Searching Questions

- Elijah used his voice and stood up for his values, even when confronted by powerful people in high places. How can you reframe your perspective from one of fear (seeing confrontation as a threat) to one of empowerment (seeing confrontation as an opportunity to advocate for positive change)?

- How can a godly confrontation support your values, assert your boundaries, and help you to cultivate a sense of courage and confidence in using your voice? What incremental steps can get you started? What truths or affirmations will help you to persist?

- How might you draw strength and inspiration from Elijah, who courageously confronted injustice and spoke truth to power? How can such stories of bravery —from Elijah, other historical figures, contemporary leaders, or individuals in your own life—motivate you to find your inner courage even when it feels like your voice won't be heard or honored?

11

Place Your Bets

When Ahab saw Elijah, Ahab said to him, "Is it you, you troubler of Israel?" He answered, "I have not troubled Israel; but you have, and your father's house, because you have forsaken the commandments of the LORD and followed the Baals. Now therefore have all Israel assemble for me at Mount Carmel, with the four hundred fifty prophets of Baal and the four hundred prophets of Asherah, who eat at Jezebel's table."

1 Kings 18:17–19

There's a well-known tradition in the sports world, and particularly in boxing, designed to intimidate one's opponents. Today it's called *trash talk*—the trading of colorful insults that stir publicity and create a psychological advantage prior to a match. Apart from expressing bravado, trash talk is meant to assert dominance and get under your adversary's skin. It sets the stage for the clash to come and increases the sense of anticipation.

Trash talk isn't new. There's an example in Scripture that involves Goliath's taunting of the Israelites. Goliath's appearance was intimidating enough, but his verbal attacks terrorized Israel's defenders. King Ahab knew a little something about intimidation too. When Elijah came out of isolation to meet with him, Ahab called Elijah the "troubler of Israel" (v. 17). The term translated "troubler" in 1 Kings 18 is *'akar* and describes the actions of someone who disrupts a community's peace and well-being.[1] Ahab's choice of words did more than accuse; he wanted to shift the blame for Israel's deteriorating state onto Elijah in hopes of undermining the prophet's authority. In reality, Ahab felt threatened by his own deteriorating reputation. He tried to give Elijah a bad name in order to save his own neck.

When blame-shifting happens, the question becomes "Who is really to blame?" Ahab and Jezebel wreaked havoc on Israel's people. Much can be said about their wicked motives and general lack of ethics. But Ahab's weakness in allowing Jezebel to speak for him and seize Naboth's vineyard was particularly egregious (1 Kings 21:1–24). Jezebel disrespected God's apportioning of land to the tribes and convinced her husband land was a mere commodity. She believed, as king, Ahab had every right to steal it. The fact she murdered Naboth further proved she and Ahab were Israel's real troublers. Their actions against Naboth sealed their fate, and Elijah proclaimed a death sentence over them (vv. 17–19, 23).

The Spaces Prophets Occupy

Israel often saw Yahweh's prophets as troublemakers and disturbers of the status quo. However, the prophets' so-called troublemaking was really a divine mission to afflict the comfortable and comfort the afflicted. Delving into the Scripture narratives of the prophets, you discover the status quo is often a façade that masks deeper societal issues. The prophets peered beyond the façades. They brought to light accepted norms and

Place Your Bets

the power differentials that separated the privileged and the oppressed.

These societal issues were significant for Yahweh and His prophets, and exposing them was risky business. Remember Hosea was dismissed as being mad, and Jeremiah was branded a traitor by court prophets who tailored their words to please the king. Of course, Ahab and Jezebel saw Elijah as a thorny and troublesome individual! Like other prophets, he was called to disrupt the deceptive peace of the status quo and guide people toward a more truthful and equitable way of living. Elijah and his prophetic peers exposed society's attempts to adopt the cultures of surrounding nations and discard the ethics and commands of Yahweh; their actions as servants of God directly opposed the political motives of the powerful.

Elijah's confrontation with King Ahab exemplifies the tension inherent within the prophet's role. When Ahab accused him of being Israel's "troubler," Elijah turned the accusation back on the king. He declared Ahab's idolatrous policies as the real source of Israel's troubles. This heated exchange resembles many of the situations we face today. Who *are* the real troublers among us? Are they the men and women who challenge us to see the truth and strive for justice? Or are they the influencers whose selfish actions disrupt the harmony we seek?

Reading the Elijah narrative should provoke other questions. Are today's prophets speaking faithfully? Or are they prophesying about everything but the testimony of Jesus, the very Spirit of Prophecy? If the church is God's prophetic witness to the world (which it is), and if the testimony of Jesus is the evidence of the Spirit of Prophecy among God's people as according to Revelation 19:10, our witness to the world is marred when the testimony of Jesus is sullied. So when the church becomes as compromised as the surrounding culture—when we speak, live, and act as the world does—can we really claim to speak for Jesus?

The truth is, we are called to bear witness to Jesus' cross-shaped life of self-sacrificial love. Paul reminded the Corinthians he determined to "know nothing . . . except Jesus Christ and him crucified" (1 Corinthians 2:2). This experiential knowing was crucial because, in many ways, the Corinthian community had betrayed the cruciform witness of Jesus, both among themselves and with outsiders. As a result, they became "troublers" for Paul and for the saints who desired to grow in the wisdom and experiential knowledge of the Crucified God.

For us to incarnate the prophetic witness, we need to address only what God is calling us to address. When we do this, peace and justice will be evident in the way we live. After all, Jesus *is* the way. This kind of living demands the deep listening and discernment that can shape our actions in ways that promote well-being and flourishing, for ourselves and the whole community. But make no mistake; this way of life is diametrically opposed to the prevailing narcissistic individualism so apparent in the current culture.

By embodying the cruciform life of Christ, we become living testimonies of His self-giving love and challenge the self-centered norms of our society. In this way, our prophetic witness to the world invites others to experience Christ's transformative power.

Continuing Clash of Worldviews

The differences between Elijah and Ahab could not have been clearer. Elijah boldly stood before the public and before Ahab's court as the prophet of Yahweh who defied his own fears to oppose the king and his wicked entourage. He tagged Ahab as the true source of Israel's trouble, and he accused the royal family of leading Israel headlong into idolatry.

In stark contrast to Elijah, Ahab was in the bloodline of Omri, one of the most decadent, compromised, and wicked

Place Your Bets

kings in Israel's history. The Omride dynasty did not bear witness to Yahweh but to their own compromised character and ethics. Even when they gave Yahweh lip service, they gave their worship to foreign gods.

Of course, Israel was a theocracy at that time. In His exaltation to the Father's right hand, Christ superseded that approach to national rule. He is now Lord of all, and whether it looks like it or not, He reigns. The question is whether we as His people are bearing witness to the One who reigns or to a facsimile that suits our own desires. Consider our words, for example. We love "lion talk," yet the Lion of the Tribe of Judah is a slain lamb. In Revelation 5:1–14, the Lamb appears in the cross-shaped position at the center of the very throne of the universe.

So why the "lion talk"? Certainly this language echoes our era. Many are ambitious for power, and they craft their words accordingly. The secular culture particularly uses "power talk" as a matter of course. But their language has crept into the church and tainted views of power within its walls. Such lingo might be deemed acceptable by some, but it is not a work of the Spirit. The power of the Holy Spirit is not self-aggrandizing and does not draw attention to self or to the gathering of power. Instead, His ways lead us to pour ourselves out and arise from the deadness of un-Christlike power structures.

The clash of worldviews typified in the clash between Ahab and Elijah is evident in two cities mentioned in the book of Revelation: the City of Fallen Man and the Bridal City of God. Whatever isn't in the Bridal City is fallen Babylon, even if it claims otherwise. If we read the sacred text faithfully, we see all earthly governments are part of Babylon. To preach against this truth is to preach a different gospel and prophesy out of a different spirit that is not the Spirit of Christ.

At an essential level, the clash is between a Christological worldview and an idolatrous worldview. The Christological view is uncompromisingly Christ-centered and cross-shaped.

From this perspective, the world was crucified to us and we are crucified to the world. Notice I didn't call it a biblical worldview—and for sound reasons. We have arrived at a point in history when we seem to make the Bible say whatever we want it to say. This is an error because the Scriptures are about Christ, who is the center of all creation. *Everything* revolves around Him.

Just as Elijah stood against Ahab during a period of widespread apostasy, we must stand against the cultural and spiritual compromises of our time. Elijah confronted the idolatry, and we must confront the false teachings and power ambitions that are distorting the gospel of Jesus Christ today. Like Elijah, who called out the false worship of Baal, we must call out the false "power talk" and self-serving ambitions that have crept into the church. We must rise out of the deadness of worldly power structures and into the life found in Christ alone.

We must discern whether we are part of the Bridal City or the City of Fallen Man. Elijah's confrontation with Ahab's idolatrous kingdom mirrors the dichotomy between the two. Earthly governments and compromised religious practices belong to fallen Babylon, even if they claim allegiance to God or are said to worship Him. A faithful reading of the sacred text ought to reveal this truth and expose what is inauthentic—but we must read faithfully. We cannot use the Scriptures to justify our personal or political agendas. The Scriptures do not disclose or endorse ideologies; they reveal Christ. We are called to bear witness to the slain Lamb who reigns. Our allegiance is not to party or nation; it is *to Him*.

Confidence of the Spirit and a Theology of Words

Elijah was not interested in trading insults with Ahab or demonstrating bravado by weaponizing accusations. However, Elijah demonstrated his unshakable faith and prophetic authority

Place Your Bets

when Ahab attempted to assert his own position at Elijah's expense. The wicked king thought Yahweh's prophet could be deterred by trash talk. However, Elijah was determined not to defend himself but to uphold the honor of Yahweh. This verbal prelude began the unfolding that was crucial to events on Mount Carmel. The veiled voice of the accuser, described in Revelation 12:10–17, spoke through Ahab and amounted to the throwing down of a gauntlet. Invisible powers used the instrument of a compromised king to make their intent known, leveraging authority over Ahab because his lust for power and appetite for evil enslaved him. Ahab was a royal puppet, and the invisible powers were his puppet masters.

Elijah understood exactly where the battle lines were drawn. He saw the powers of hell defying the God of Angel Armies, and words mattered. His exchange with Ahab was the visible stage on which invisible realities unfolded. Ahab's accusation served as the opening salvo in what became one of the most revealing spiritual battles in Scripture. To this day, the events at Mount Carmel live in the memory of Israel and the church.

In all of Elijah's interactions with Ahab and Baal, evident is the timeless power of words to intimidate, challenge, and reveal truth. Where I grew up, we had a special term for verbal confrontation. We called it *wolf talk*. Not idle chatter, this clear and unambiguous warning announced a fight was coming, a fierce and primal challenge that demanded a response. Both sides knew the stakes, and both had to be ready to stand their ground.

In the narrative of Ahab and Elijah, the king's accusatory words are like the fierce growls of a predator asserting dominance. Elijah's response is the resolute roar of a prophet who stands firm in God's truth. A theology of words is therefore significant as an understanding of why words matter and how the word needs to be understood from a theological framework, to see how language and speech are viewed and utilized in sacred contexts, particularly in relation to their divine significance and impact on human life.

In the sacred text, God creates the world through speech. Genesis 1 repeatedly states, "And God said," highlighting creation as an act of divine utterance. John 1:1 refers to Jesus Christ as the Word, *Logos*. The incarnation, in which the Word became flesh, stresses the essential connection between divine communication and human existence. Jesus embodies the ultimate expression of God's message to humanity.

In the Scriptures, prophets such as Elijah speak God's words to His people. Such speech carries divine authority and often challenges injustice, idolatry, and unfaithfulness. Prophetic speech is seen as a conduit for God's will and truth. The Scriptures also provide ethical guidelines on the use of words. Proverbs 18:21 states, "Death and life are in the power of the tongue," meaning words can harm or heal, bless or curse. Therefore, ethical speech is rooted in the truth, love, and justice that reflect God's character.

The same is true of the words we speak in worship, prayer, and communal gatherings. Words are central to our sacred practices. Liturgical speech shapes our faith community's identity and relationship with God. Our recitation of Scripture, hymns, prayers, and creeds constitutes a collective expression of belief. Confessing our faith and bearing witness to God's work are vital aspects of Christian life. Testimonies of God's grace and intervention are powerful affirmations of faith.

Words also play a crucial role in healing relationships and fostering reconciliation. Apologies, forgiveness, and words of affirmation can mend broken relationships and reflect God's reconciling work in Christ. In essence, a theology of words recognizes language as a divine gift with profound implications. A theology of words calls us as believers to use words responsibly and reverently, discerning their potential to reflect divine truth and bring about transformation.

A Spirituality of Words

What about a spirituality of words? As image-bearers, we live in language as well as emotions, feelings, and moods, all of which we embody. Words have power to shape reality, influence decisions, and alter the course of history. They carry the ability to build up or tear down, to heal or to wound.

A spirituality of words recognizes our speech is an extension of our inner lives and spiritual states. Words are not merely sounds or symbols; they are carriers of meaning and intention. In the biblical narrative, God speaks creation into existence, demonstrating the foundational power of divine speech. As creatures made in God's image, our words also possess creative potential and can bring forth life or death in our interactions.

The truth of God backs up Elijah's words. Therefore, his words revealed the divine authority and prophetic courage to confront falsehood. Elijah's speech was an act of faithfulness aligned with God's will and purpose. Elijah's bold declaration against Ahab was not a mere personal challenge but a spiritual act that called Israel back to covenant faithfulness. The things he said underscored the role words play in spiritual warfare and moral confrontation.

Conversely, Ahab's words seemed charged with royal authority but were empty and deceptive. They represented the misuse of language, meant to manipulate, distort, and lead others astray. His language reveals the glaring difference between the truth of God and the lies of idolaters. Ahab's words reflected a heart far from God. They showed how corrupt speech can propagate falsehood and injustice.

The confrontation between Elijah and Ahab reminds us of the sobering responsibility we have when we speak. Our speech should reflect the character of God by being truthful, just, and loving. The spirituality of words calls us to be mindful that every spoken word can either align us with divine truth or lead us into moral and spiritual compromise. As followers of Christ, we are called to speak life, uphold justice, and embody the truth in all our communications.

All of these truths would be typified in Elijah's next confrontation with Ahab—the dramatic showdown on Mount Carmel.

When Worldviews Clash

When Elijah confronted Obadiah with a dangerous mission, Obadiah questioned Elijah regarding the danger involved. Yet Obadiah accepted his mission. He "went to meet Ahab, and told him; and Ahab went to meet Elijah" (1 Kings 18:16). When Ahab accused Elijah of troubling Israel, Elijah corrected and instructed the king with very plain, authoritative speech.

> I have not troubled Israel, but you have, and your father's house, because you have forsaken the commandments of the LORD and followed the Baals. Now therefore have all Israel assemble for me at Mount Carmel, with the four hundred fifty prophets of Baal and the four hundred prophets of Asherah, who eat at Jezebel's table.
>
> 1 Kings 18:18–19

The stage had been set, and the matter was soon to be settled. Elijah and Ahab and their respective worldviews prepared to go head-to-head. The Mount Carmel showdown would be the prophetic speech-act of a solitary and reclusive Tishbite against a multitude, words of truth spoken to contradict words of falsehood, the work of faith against idolatry. Elijah's confrontation with Ahab would be a testament to the enduring power of prophetic courage and divine truth.

The divine theater at Mount Carmel illustrated the spiritual struggle the Elijah-Ahab conflict represented. Everything about the showdown was meaningful. The scene was possibly chosen

Place Your Bets

for its convenience, but its status as a high place was significant, and the divine presence was about to be felt by all who gathered there. Perhaps the place was known as a "vineyard of God," symbolizing fertility.[2] Whatever the case might be, Elijah stood before the people, expecting the confrontation to force them into making the decision they had long avoided.

Once "Ahab sent to all the Israelites, and assembled the prophets at Mount Carmel" (v. 20), "Elijah . . . came near to all the people, and said, 'How long will you go limping with two different opinions? If the LORD is God, follow him; but if Baal, then follow him' . . . [but] the people did not answer him a word" (v. 21).

Elijah made the issue clear enough. You could say the people had been halting, or "hobbling on crutches," trying to serve Yahweh and Baal at the same time. The prophet insisted their dual loyalty betrayed any true faith they claimed. In fact, the two different opinions they tried to straddle were mutually exclusive, and Elijah compelled them to choose one or the other.

Their silence speaks volumes about their resistance to making this crucial decision. Their reticence might be psychological as well as theological. Specifically, they likely feared the wrath of Ahab. At the same time, they were surely aware of their foolishness in lying against the truth. They would either serve Ahab and Baal or they would serve Yahweh. To continue serving both was a violation of their psyches, promoting internal imbalance and potential long-term deleterious consequences.

Rules of Engagement

Elijah had thrown down a gauntlet as well and was about to establish the rules of the contest to an audience that had so far chosen to remain silent. Elijah was meticulous about the details he presented. Bulls were chosen, and because Baal was believed to preside over fire, Elijah established fire as the deciding factor of the contest. The ground rules were clear, eliminating any doubt when the final results were tabulated.

> Elijah said to the people, "I, even I only, am left a prophet of the LORD; but Baal's prophets number four hundred fifty. Let two bulls be given to us; let them choose one bull for themselves, cut it in pieces, and lay it on the wood, but put no fire to it. I will prepare the other bull and lay it on the wood, but put no fire to it. Then you call on the name of your god and I will call on the name of the LORD; the god who answers by fire is indeed God."
>
> 1 Kings 18:22–24

Although it would seem unthinkable for the people to choose against Yahweh, Elijah knew that choosing Him to the exclusion of Baal would be a radical and costly decision for them—perhaps a life-or-death decision. If they continued to be lukewarm, they might escape Ahab and Jezebel's wrath, but God would spit them out of His mouth (Revelation 3:16). The people's response to Elijah's invitation was encouraging. They simply shouted, "Well spoken!" (v. 24).

It's Baal's Turn

Once the prophets of Baal had prepared their bull, they began to call on their god, "from morning until noon." They cried, "'O Baal, answer us!' But there was no voice and no answer . . . [so] they limped about the altar that they had made" (v. 26).

At noon, Elijah injected some trash talk of his own. He mocked Baal and his prophets, saying, "Cry aloud! Surely he is a god; either he is meditating, or he has wandered away, or he is on a journey, or perhaps he is asleep and must be awakened" (v. 27). The Hebrew text reveals deeper nuances, suggesting Baal might be "relieving himself" (שִׂיג).[3] The mention of bodily functions was an intentional insult, implying Baal was not only absent but detained by mundane human functions.

Place Your Bets

Elijah's mockery sharply contrasted Baal's impotence with the divine power that would soon be powerfully demonstrated. Baal's prophets were in a desperate situation.

> They cried aloud [again] and, as was their custom, they cut themselves with swords and lances until the blood gushed out over them. As midday passed, they raved on until the time of the offering of the oblation, but there was no voice, no answer, and no response.
>
> 1 Kings 18:28–29

Baal remained unresponsive to the false prophets' cries. Although Jezebel was not physically present (an interesting detail we will soon explore), her influence loomed large, and the prophets of Baal made ever more passionate appeals to their god. Frantic to elicit a response, they resorted to self-mutilation. More than a display of their devotion, this cutting revealed their deep psychological distress and the emptiness of their faith in a god who remained indifferent and unresponsive to them.

In their despair, they presumed inflicting pain upon themselves would prove their sincerity and perhaps compel their god to act. This act of utter hopelessness could also be understood as an attempt to exert control in a situation over which they felt powerless. However, their actions only underscored the futility of their faith, or more correctly, their pseudo-faith, and the powerlessness of Baal. Amid this hollow and tragic display, Elijah stood by, confident Yahweh's faithfulness and responsiveness would soon be seen.

The Lessons of Idolatry

The portion of the 1 Kings 18 narrative we have covered so far is a kind of textbook case about the ills of idolatry. It particularly raises questions about Jezebel's absence, her prophets' self-mutilation, and the workings of idolatry, all of which are relevant to the contemporary church.

Jezebel's Absence

Jezebel's failure to attend the showdown is both curious and striking. As an immensely powerful queen who never hesitated to proclaim Baal and slaughter Yahweh's prophets, she would be hard-pressed to explain her failure to show up when her gods were challenged.

From the perspective of depth psychology, her absence revealed a deeper, unconscious recognition of the power struggle in play. Despite her bullying and bombast, she might have entertained underlying doubts about Baal's power. Her nonappearance could be seen as a defense mechanism, a way to avoid a confrontation that might expose Baal's impotence and her own vulnerability.

From a philosophical standpoint, Jezebel's absence could be interpreted as an act of strategic avoidance. Assuming she understood the symbolic nature of the contest (it's hard to believe she didn't), she might have chosen not to dignify it with her presence. Showing disdain and refusing to directly engage in Elijah's challenge could have been interpreted as Jezebel's way of staying above the fray and maintaining control.

A realist might argue Jezebel's absence was a calculated political move. By not appearing, she could avoid the potential fallout of a public defeat. If Baal's prophets were to fail, her absence would allow her to manage the risk, distance herself from the immediate humiliation, regroup, and maintain her influence and power.

From a prophetic perspective, could Jezebel's absence be seen as a divine orchestration? Her nonappearance certainly seemed to underscore the powerlessness of Baal and Asherah. With the queen out of sight, God could demonstrate His supremacy

Place Your Bets

without any of the distraction or interference she would have injected. The focus was more squarely set on the true source of Israel's troubles and on Elijah's call to faithfulness.

The Prophets' Self-Mutilation

In their despair, the prophets' cutting of their own flesh was an extreme way of coping with overwhelming emotions. They tried to bridge the chasm between Baal's silence and their suffering. However, their bloodletting only brought that void and the contrast between the living God and false idols into sharper focus. Their self-destructive behavior can be seen as a metaphor for how idolatry ultimately harms the worshiper. When we turn to false gods in the hope of finding meaning or gratification, we often sacrifice our well-being, our relationships, and our integrity.

The false prophets' actions also reflected a gross misunderstanding of the nature of the divine. They believed their god required extreme measures to appease them or convince them to act. The God of Israel demands no such measures. He simply desires mercy, justice, and humility from us. This contrast speaks to a broader theological truth. The true God does not require our harm; He seeks our flourishing and wholeness.

Finally, the prophets' self-mutilation is a poignant reminder of our human attempts to control the divine or transcendent. The prophets of Baal tried to manipulate their god. This failed attempt mirrors the tendency of people in our time to address their feelings of powerlessness or abandonment by trying to control their lives or destinies through unhealthy or extreme behaviors. This kind of desperation springs from a deep spiritual hunger and a misplaced understanding of how to commune with God the Father of our Lord Jesus Christ.

The desperate prophets' plight calls us to reflect on the objects of our devotion. Are we trying to elicit responses from lifeless idols, such as material possessions, status, or false ideologies? Or are we fully invested in the living God, who hears our cries and responds with love and power? Are we participating in popular forms of faith that deemphasize a transformative relationship with God and treat the church and spirituality as commodities to be consumed? Or are we feeding on Christ by His Spirit?

Instead of being characterized by a sacrificial commitment to Christ and His mission, much of the church is focused on personal satisfaction, convenience, and the pursuit of blessings. Just as the prophets of Baal cried out to an unresponsive deity, many today find themselves turning to things that promise peace where there is no peace (Jeremiah 6:14).

There is also a widespread tendency to disregard appropriate discernment, even by embracing prophetic utterances that promise much but offer little of the substance that belongs to Christ. This can leave the saints feeling manipulated by the prophetic, leaving them feeling empty and unheard.

In the end, true fulfillment comes not from fleshly prophetism, worthless idols, or the consumption of spiritual goods. It comes from a deep, abiding relationship with the God who hears our cries and responds with grace and power. This is exactly what Elijah understood, and this truth defined how he lived. Throughout the confrontation on Mount Carmel, he was composed and confident. And as the prophets of Baal came apart at the seams, almost literally, Elijah stood firm in the knowledge of his God and the anticipation of what would come next.

Soul-Searching Questions

- When faced with false accusations, how can you follow Christ's example of responding with wisdom, grace, and a refusal to return evil for evil? What scriptural principles can guide you amid the injustice?

Place Your Bets

- Consider how Elijah likely wrestled with his emotions when Ahab falsely accused him at a critical point in Israel's history and in his own life. How can scriptural truths and strategies help you to manage your anger, shame, or other difficult feelings that false charges can trigger?

- Elijah saw his confrontation with Ahab for what it was: a clash of worldviews, with faith and idolatry as opposite poles. How might discerning this common dichotomy guide your conduct when similar clashes arise, whether at a more intimate, interpersonal level or in larger settings?

12

Restoring the Altar of the Lord

Elijah said to all the people, "Come closer to me"; and all the people came closer to him. First he repaired the altar of the LORD that had been thrown down.

1 Kings 18:30

When it became clear Baal could not answer his prophets, it was Elijah's turn to act. In the stillness of the moment, he told the people, "Come closer to me" (1 Kings 18:30). This was more than a simple request; it was a divine summons to draw near to him and, more importantly, to God. As Elijah's voice rang out, it cut through the noise of doubt and distraction. The people responded by drawing near to the prophet.

Elijah's invitation at that moment speaks to the human spiritual journey today. It invites us to seek intimacy with God and leave behind the chaos of our lives. It draws us out of our confusion and into spaces where we can hear the Lord's heart, intent, and voice. Elijah urged the Israelites to enter such a space. Although they would soon witness a stunning miracle, he

181

hoped they would also enter a deeper relationship with God—one built on trust, faith, and obedience.

First Things First

As the people gathered around Elijah, he maintained a big-picture perspective about a moment freighted in history and future hopes. He had waited patiently, knowing the Baals would never show up. Now he could prepare the way for what the living God had in mind. So Elijah began with the sacred task of restoring what had been destroyed during Ahab's reign.

> First he repaired the altar of the LORD that had been thrown down; Elijah took twelve stones, according to the number of the tribes of the sons of Jacob, to whom the word of the LORD came, saying, "Israel shall be your name"; with the stones he built an altar in the name of the LORD.
>
> 1 Kings 18:30–32

This act of restoration was a symbolic and physical manifestation of the spiritual renewal God intended. Using twelve stones representing the twelve tribes of Israel, Elijah rebuilt the altar in the name of the Lord. This act of rebuilding reminded Israel of the covenant God had made with them—a covenant they had neglected and even forgotten.

It is easy to imagine the people standing in a collective hush, eyes fixed on Elijah's every move as he put each stone in place. His meticulous rebuilding of the altar was a prophetic act intended to stir the depths of their consciousness and spark their memory, as a people and as individuals. In the silence, a shift from distraction to deep awareness became possible. The resulting state of heightened consciousness allowed them to perceive the significance of Elijah's actions in ways they might not have previously considered.

Restoring the Altar of the Lord

The question becomes whether the observers stood as passive witnesses or active participants in a sacred drama. Was their awareness drawn inward? Did it prompt them to reflect on their own spiritual state? The selection of twelve stones could not have gone unnoticed, even by spiritually dull Jews. The number of the tribes of Israel served to stir their collective memory of identity and covenant with God. This realization came with conviction and godly sorrow and a reminder of what Moses had declared prophetically at Sinai:

> Now therefore, if you obey my voice and keep my covenant, you shall be my treasured possession out of all the peoples. Indeed, the whole earth is mine, but you shall be for me a priestly kingdom and a holy nation. These are the words that you shall speak to the Israelites.
>
> Exodus 19:5–6

Attuned to the Israelites' history with God, Elijah beckoned the people to see beyond the stones and perceive what they symbolized—a call to holiness, renewal of their divine mission, and restoration of their confidence in God's unwavering commitment. This collective remembering of identity and calling was meant to inspire spiritual renewal and communal solidarity for God's chosen people.

A Heady Experience

To think about what the people experienced inwardly as they watched Elijah's very intentional and painstaking actions, we must consider what they actually saw and how they saw it. I am referring to their *phenomenology*, "the study of structures of consciousness as experienced from the first-person point of view."[1] The term, originally used in the eighteenth century, is integral to the modern philosophy of phenomenology that studies human experiences exactly as they occur.[2]

To consider the inner experiences of the people who watched Elijah on Mount Carmel, we can look further and ask what exactly they were perceiving. This is more than the physical act of seeing; it includes how each person processed and understood the sensory information presented in the situation. The observers' perceptions were shaped not only by what they saw but by their beliefs, emotions, and past experiences. This suggests a tendency to see Elijah's actions as deeply significant acts tied to their faith, culture, and personal expectations. As a result, the people could have experienced a range of responses, from awe and conviction to confusion and skepticism.

It is difficult not to wonder about Elijah's inner experience at this point. Was his hope tied to the effect of this teaching moment? I suspect it was. He may well have hoped the people's observing would become a form of meditation—a way to connect or reconnect with the deeper truths of their faith. Watching Elijah rebuild the altar was a good opportunity to bracket out everyday concerns and enter a state of spiritual contemplation. This conscious bracketing, as described in phenomenological studies,[3] offered the potential for observers to experience the Mount Carmel event in its purest form, free from preconceived notions and distractions.

Elijah's well-chosen acts built a heightened form of awareness essential to the people's discerning of what was really happening. His intentionality and prophetic deeds were intended to move the people beyond mere intellectual understanding. He wanted them to grasp a direct, intuitive sense of the moment's spiritual significance. He wanted them to know his activity was not only about repairing a physical structure but about calling them back to the way of being they had buried under layers of neglect and forgetfulness.

This was an ontological shift, a fundamental change in the way the people understood who they were and why they were

Restoring the Altar of the Lord

who they were. It was a call to remember their true nature as God's people, to listen deeply to the voice of the Spirit, and to act according to divine guidance. In this sacred space, they could discern God's thoughts and ways apart from the noise of their lives. They could once again cultivate a posture of openness and receptivity and become attuned to the Spirit's ways.

Such discernment far exceeded the making of wise decisions; it was about the people subjecting their entire beings to the divine will. Elijah's prophetic enactment was a form of instruction. As a result, they were expected to be wise and regain understanding by remembering "the fear of the LORD is the beginning of wisdom, and the knowledge of the Holy One is insight" (Proverbs 9:10).

Those of us who are in Christ can understand this event from the perspective of what the incarnation has revealed in Jesus' personhood and work; His death, burial, resurrection, and ascension; and the outpouring of the Spirit at Pentecost. True wisdom is now embraced from the inside out through the indwelling Spirit of Christ. There is therefore what we could call an inner knowing of Christ. This is Christ in us, who is the hope of our ultimate glorification and who, by the working of grace, enables us to transcend our intellectual limits and receive from the infinite reservoir of God's own mind.

The events on Mount Carmel reminded God's people that observation and awareness are not passive acts but powerful tools for spiritual growth. By being fully present and attentive, they could discern the deeper meanings of their life experiences and respond with faith and wisdom. Elijah offered the people a renewed way of being with a restored sense of original intentionality. Instead of limping between two decisions (1 Kings 18:21), they could walk in the light of God's presence and make every moment count.

Like the people Elijah called to "come closer," we are called to repair the altars of our hearts. Let's "come closer" and examine the places where our faith has been broken down or our relationship with God has been neglected. It's time to restore what has been lost and rebuild our spiritual lives on the foundation of God's promises.

Water, Water Everywhere

With the altar repairs done, Elijah continued his intentional, meticulous preparations. "He made a trench around the altar, large enough to contain two measures of seed. Next he put the wood in order, cut the bull in pieces, and laid it on the wood" (1 Kings 18:32–33).

Then Elijah made sure the results of the contest would be irrefutable.

> He said, "Fill four jars with water and pour it on the burnt offering and on the wood." Then he said, "Do it a second time"; and they did it a second time. Again he said, "Do it a third time"; and they did it a third time, so that the water ran all around the altar, and filled the trench also with water.
>
> 1 Kings 18:33–35

Elijah ordered the burnt offering to be doused not once but three times, so the water ran completely around the altar and filled the trench. This liberal use of water seemed extravagant in a time of drought. The average water jar contained three and a half gallons. Twelve jars held at least forty-two gallons of the precious commodity, enough water to keep a family of four supplied for as many as twenty-one days! Elijah wasn't being wasteful, however. He was proclaiming his radical faith and the gravity of the moment. He sacrificed the water to demonstrate God's power and sovereignty, making his challenge to the prophets of Baal even more impactful. This dramatic act was based on Elijah's radical trust in God and the miraculous nature of God's coming response. His trust showed true worship involves offering even our most precious resources to God, believing He will provide.

Still, a question lingers in my mind. Where did all that water come from? Did Elijah know of a hidden spring in the mountain or have some nearby secret source? No one can say. Given Mount Carmel's proximity to the Mediterranean Sea, it's possible seawater was used. However, using salt water does not make sense because within the context of Holy Writ, only fresh water symbolizes purity, life, cleansing, and covenant blessing. Drenching the altar with fresh water emphasized the purity of true worship and the life-giving power of the one true God. Ultimately, Elijah's use of water served as a visual reminder of God's covenant faithfulness.

One thing is certain. Elijah's copious pouring of water over the sacrifice constituted his direct defiance of King Ahab. Both men and all the observers knew extreme soaking of the sacrifice would make burning it impossible. If the fire did manage to consume it, there would be no refuting the miracle of God. The One who had the power to stop the rain also had the power to bring fire and burn everything in its path.

When Lightning Strikes, Fire Falls

As the sun set over Mount Carmel and twilight deepened, a hushed anticipation fell over the crowd. The oblation—the daily time of the evening prayer and sacrifice (Exodus 29:38–39)—was upon them in an extraordinary way. The oblation marked the transition from day to night and served as a time of reflecting on the day's events. The faithful in Israel gave daily thanks for that day's blessings, sought forgiveness for any transgressions they may have committed, and sought divine protection and blessing for the ensuing night season.

The evening prayer was a personal act of devotion and a communal activity that helped to reinforce the Israelites' sense of community. It is unlikely the people underwent the ceremonial washing of ritual purification on Mount Carmel. Yet approaching God together in prayer was a sacred act, with protocols that Israel was called to follow. The evening prayers likely included psalms, blessings, and petitions. Psalm 141:2 captures the attitude of such prayer times and offers one's heart and intentions to God, stating, "Let my prayer be counted as incense before you, and the lifting up of my hands as an evening sacrifice."

Priests played a crucial role, acting as intermediaries between the people and God and ensuring the rituals were performed correctly. Elijah served as a singular priest and prophet on Mount Carmel. When he entered the established sacred significance of evening prayer, he not only called for divine intervention but also aligned with the daily rhythm of Israelite worship, making his plea even more resonant with the people.

As Elijah stood before the altar and lifted his voice, his words carried across the silent crowd. He began his prayer saying, "O Yahweh, God of Abraham, Isaac, and Israel," invoking the patriarchs in a rare and powerful manner. He was doing more than invoking Israel's heritage; this was a direct call to the God who had covenanted with their ancestors. So Elijah continued, saying, "Let it be known today that you are God in Israel" (1 Kings 18:36 LEB).

I can imagine how the word *today* hung in the air, adding a sense of immediacy and conveying to the crowd the gravity of Elijah's request. They had seen the frantic cries of Baal's prophets throughout the day. They saw how those cries availed nothing but the letting of human blood. Now, whether they believed it or not, they stood on the brink of witnessing real power—the power of Yahweh.

Elijah's voice rose again. "Answer me, O Yahweh, answer me," he implored (v. 37). This straightforward plea contrasted starkly with the empty rituals of Baal's prophets. Elijah's prayer

Restoring the Altar of the Lord

called for more than divine fire; he longed for the people's hearts to be turned back to Yahweh.

As Elijah finished praying, the air thick with tension, every eye was on the altar. Suddenly, a bolt of lightning—a fiery manifestation of Yahweh's presence—struck the sacrifice. The fire consumed everything: the offering, the wood, the stones, the dust, and even the water in the trench. The completeness of the destruction manifested an awe-inspiring expression of Yahweh's absolute power. At the sight of this miraculous display, the onlookers fell to their faces. As one body, they acknowledged the utter and inexorable supremacy of Yahweh. "Yahweh, he is God! Yahweh, he is God!" they cried, their voices echoing Elijah's declaration (v. 39). A certain irony is not lost in the people's reaction. They needed to see the fire fall before they themselves could fall in worship. By consuming the altar completely, God ensured it would never be used again. God's act of consuming the stone itself accentuated the totality of His power and the seriousness of maintaining pure and obedient worship according to His commandments.

This unanimous acknowledgment of Yahweh's supremacy was meant to be Israel's turning point. We discover later that it wasn't. Yet in this moment on Mount Carmel, the people's response comports with how they historically responded to God in crises, from their days in the wilderness all the way through their days in the land God gave them. Yet not many years after this showdown, they would be exiled and scattered. Both the Northern and Southern Kingdoms would grieve over what they lost because they forgot God and experienced the agonizing consequences of their forgetting.

The Slaughter of the False Prophets

I have mentioned the prophets of Baal, but the prophets of Asherah were also present on Mount Carmel. Baal's prophets numbered 450; Asherah's numbered 400; and all of these so-called prophets ate at Jezebel's table (1 Kings 18:19).

The prophets' vast numbers stemmed from several factors. Firstly, the political and religious influence of Ahab and Jezebel required a strong public presence. The prophets served not only as spiritual leaders but as instruments of the royal agenda, ensuring the widespread acceptance and practice of Baal and Asherah worship throughout the kingdom. The greater their presence, the better the message of religious dominance could be enforced. Rituals and ceremonies dedicated to Baal and Asherah were also many and complex. Ahab and Jezebel needed large numbers of priests and prophets to lead the people in worship, maintain temples, and ensure the cults' influence by performing their intricate rituals.

Jezebel's support and patronage were key to funding the training and maintenance of these prophets. Temples were built and resources allocated to ensure the prophets were well-equipped and protected. It seems likely many of the prophets were integrated from existing local traditions and neighboring cultures where Baal and Asherah worship was already prevalent. This cultural integration expanded the cult's influence, as did the likely charisma and personal appeal that helped some of the prophets gain recognition and attract followers. Their purported spiritual experiences and miracles also reinforced the royal religious agenda.

In this context, the large number of prophets reflected more than a sense of religious devotion. They revealed a calculated strategy by Ahab and Jezebel to control and indoctrinate the populace. The prophets of Baal and Asherah were pivotal in shaping Israel's religious landscape. They ensured the worship of idols was deeply embedded in the culture and politics of the time.

It is perhaps no surprise that Elijah had strong feelings about the false prophets. No sooner had the fire fallen, consuming

Restoring the Altar of the Lord

the entire sacrifice and altar, that Elijah addressed the people again, saying, "Seize the prophets of Baal; do not let one of them escape" (v. 40). The people did what Elijah asked and seized the prophets. Then Elijah led the captured prophets from Mount Carmel down to the Wadi Kishon, in the Jezreel Valley, and there he slaughtered them by the edge of the sword.[4]

The Hebrew word *šāḥaṭ* (translated "slaughter") in 1 Kings 18:40 depersonalizes the Baal prophets and likens their deaths to those of slaughtered animals. Jezebel had already cut off the prophets of the Lord by the edge of the sword. Now Elijah directs what seems to be an unauthorized slaughter of Jezebel's prophets. As the late Walter Brueggemann wrote, "The episode underscores the severity of the issue and the lack of any sense of compassion."[5]

How are we to understand this event in light of Christ and our contemporary perspective? In the ancient Near Eastern context, religious and cultural conflicts were intense. The use of a verb indicating slaughter accentuates the deep divide between the worship and worshipers of Yahweh and those of Baal. The use of such a term contrasts Elijah's decisive action with Jezebel's more targeted and sinister persecution of Yahweh's prophets. It also contrasts the comprehensive nature of Elijah's purge with Jezebel's personal vendetta.

Elijah's moral compass in this regard was likely guided by the death penalty prescribed for idolators (see Deuteronomy 7:2–6; 13:13–15; 17:2–5). When he instructed the people, who had just confessed that Yahweh is God, they responded instantly. From a theological perspective, this was divine justice. The prophets of Baal had led the people astray. The very people who had fallen prey to their seductive lies now judged and executed them—a drastic measure seemingly commensurate with the seriousness of idolatry and the need for true worship.

In his moment of triumph, Elijah showed he could match the resolve and severity of his adversaries, reflecting the intense and often brutal nature of the spiritual and political conflicts of his time. However, we need to transition from Elijah's time to our current understanding in Christ. From this vantage point, we recognize we have come to the fullness of times and a more complete revelation of God and His ways. Jesus has invited us to consider a greater reality that emphasizes mercy, love, and forgiveness. Let's explore this shift through other scriptural insights. When Judas betrayed Jesus in Gethsemane, Jesus had already determined to test His disciples in relation to their higher calling in Him. Judas seemed unprepared for the test.

> At once he came up to Jesus and said, "Greetings, Rabbi!" and kissed him. Jesus said to him, "Friend, do what you are here to do." Then they came and laid hands on Jesus and arrested him. Suddenly, one of those with Jesus put his hand on his sword, drew it, and struck the slave of the high priest, cutting off his ear. Then Jesus said to him, "Put your sword back into its place; for all who take the sword will perish by the sword."
>
> Matthew 26:49–52

Jesus taught His disciples a new and different way that transcends the retributive justice of Elijah's time.

> He said to [the disciples], "When I sent you out without a purse, bag, or sandals, did you lack anything?" They said, "No, not a thing." He said to them, "But now, the one who has a purse must take it, and likewise a bag. And the one who has no sword must sell his cloak and buy one. For I tell you, this scripture must be fulfilled in me, 'And he was counted among the lawless'; and indeed what is written about me is being fulfilled." They said, "Lord, look, here are two swords." He replied, "It is enough."
>
> Luke 22:35–38

When Jesus said, "It is enough," He wasn't talking about the right number of swords. He was gently rebuking His disciples for their misunderstanding. They failed to grasp that He was speaking metaphorically of the spiritual and physical trials they would face with Him. Jesus was warning them to prepare for the hardships of following Him, entering into His sufferings, and sharing in His mission. He wanted them to know that His kingdom was not about violence but about enduring suffering and standing firm in faith.

Luke Timothy Johnson shares certain insights into these matters. Jesus began His ministry declaring the fulfillment of Isaiah's prophecy and ends by stating that another Scripture from Isaiah must be completed in Him. This shows continuity in Jesus' mission. The term "counted among the lawless" in Luke 22:37 suggests that Jesus' death was not a human plot but part of God's divine plan, fulfilling Isaiah's prophecy of the Suffering Servant. Jesus' innocent suffering serves to atone for the sins of others. The disciples' misunderstanding about the need for swords reveals their unpreparedness and confusion about Jesus' mission. They respond violently in the garden, showing they still do not grasp Jesus' teachings on peace and nonviolence.[6]

Jesus' message was clear. Though they might need to prepare for trials and opposition, violence was not the answer. In Christ, the fullness of God's revelation teaches us to discern the Spirit's guidance, act in love, and pursue peace.

In today's culture, violence is on the rise and words easily escalate into rage. We need to heed these texts and the voice of the Spirit within them and be exhorted to listen attentively to what the Spirit is saying. The Spirit calls us to embody Christ's teachings in our lives—to seek justice, love mercy, and walk humbly with our God. In every challenge and conflict, may we discern the higher calling of Christ, embrace His way of peace and reconciliation, and act accordingly.

May we, like Elijah, stand firm in our faith, but with the understanding that in Christ we are called to a transformative and redemptive love that reflects the true nature of God.

Soul-Searching Questions

- Reflect on how Elijah carefully rebuilt the altar with twelve stones, representing the unity of Israel's twelve tribes. What areas of fragmentation or disunity in your life need to be restored and rebuilt? What intentional steps can you take to present a unified "altar" before the Lord, aligning your thoughts, desires, and actions with His will?

- Elijah's bold actions in rebuilding the altar and calling upon the Lord were rooted in his unwavering faith and obedience. In what ways have you allowed fear, doubt, or disobedience to hinder your ability to boldly seek the Lord's intervention in your life? What barriers or hindrances need to be removed so you can position yourself for the fire of the Spirit to fall?

- Elijah prayed with a heart fully surrendered, presenting himself as a living sacrifice before the Lord. In your prayer life, what areas have you held back from full surrender to God? What might it look like for you to present your entire being—your thoughts, desires, relationships, and future—as a living sacrifice, trusting in the Lord's power to consume and transform you?

13

Is It Rain That I Hear?

Elijah said to Ahab, "Go up, eat and drink; for there is a sound
of rushing rain."

1 Kings 18:41

At the top of Mount Carmel, Elijah shifted his attention from
the violent mass defeat of the prophets of Baal to a one-on-one
interaction with King Ahab. The king knew he had been publicly
defeated and exposed as impotent. So when Elijah instructed
him to "Go up, eat and drink" (1 Kings 18:41), Ahab obeyed.

Elijah's instructions were notably devoid of anger and vili-
fication, but the idea of a feast could seem out of place after
the slaughter of Baal's prophets. Elijah was not inappropriate,
however; he was calling for a different kind of feast in a certain
kind of moment. This was a time of potential covenant renewal
and divine encounter, and Elijah acted accordingly.

Biblically speaking, the prophet's instructions were laden
with meaning. In Scripture, "eating and drinking" often marks

195

the celebration of life (Ecclesiastes 8:15). The phrase is deeply covenantal, harking back to Mount Sinai, where Moses and the seventy elders beheld God and ate and drank in His presence (Exodus 24:9–11). However, Jesus once warned about certain eating and drinking that happened in Noah's time. God's people were thoroughly engrossed in merriment, oblivious to impending judgment (Matthew 24:37–39).

Yet even when His image-bearers are deep in compromise and evil, God yearns to eat and drink with them. This desire is ultimately tied to the sacramental meal of the Eucharist, in which Jesus declares the bread and wine to be His body and blood. Similarly, Elijah's invitation to Ahab anticipated not just physical nourishment but spiritual renewal. There was also an expectation of rain, a sign of God's blessing and restoration. Remarkably, Elijah heard the rain before even a cloud appeared or a word of prayer was uttered. He was not hearing with physical ears but with ears of faith.

Elijah was attuned to the God who calls things that are not as though they are (Romans 4:17)—the God who calls us from the future to the future. Elijah was watching for subtle but powerful glimpses of what was to come. He heard the impending deluge that would break three and a half years of drought. A blessing beyond measure was headed their way.

Elijah's spiritual senses were trained to discern good and evil (Hebrews 5:14), making him able to perceive what the Spirit was revealing (John 16:13). On Mount Carmel, he embodied the prayer of Matthew 6:10, which in the Greek reads, "Kingdom, come!" Years of attuned listening and intercession had sharpened Elijah's hearing of God's voice. He was prepared to hear the rain that had not yet come. He understood that it signaled the drought's end. His experience demonstrated the inbreaking of the future into the present, reminding us that "faith comes by hearing, and hearing through the word about Christ" (Romans 10:17 LEB).

Is It Rain That I Hear?

In his innermost being, Elijah knew that God intended for the rain to fall. It would fall on the "just and the unjust" alike (Matthew 5:45 NKJV), in keeping with God's impartiality and abundant grace. By the time Elijah arrived at the feast, the tables had been turned and Ahab took his seat under Elijah's order.

It Starts with Silence

The spiritual formation that prepared Elijah to hear the rain was marked by silence, stillness, and beholding, key practices emphasized by Maggie Ross in her marvelous work *Silence*.[1] Throughout Elijah's time in solitary places, he cultivated an abiding stillness within which God's voice became clearer to him. The prophet's repeated forays into solitude were more than escapes; they were essential practices that emptied him of distractions by the inner working of the Spirit. They quieted his being and attuned his spirit to God's subtle promptings.

Ross explains that becoming a person in the fullest sense of the word and realizing our shared nature with God involves radical shifts in perception and reality.[2] This was evident in Elijah's ability to hear what was inaudible to others. In the times of silence and stillness, when Elijah learned to behold the glory of the Lord, he was transformed "from one degree of glory to another" (2 Corinthians 3:18). His deep inner knowing and spiritual senses became so finely tuned that he perceived what others could not.

The connection between silence, stillness, and divine revelation is essential. According to Ross, true transformation happens as we learn to be silent and still, mirroring God's outpouring of Himself. This is not just a path to glory; it is glory itself.[3] Elijah embodied this truth as he listened, discerned, and acted on the Spirit's promptings. Because of his disciplined practices, Elijah was present to all that the moment of inbreaking required of him.

In the same way, we are called to cultivate silence and stillness in our own lives. Then we can become more attuned to the Spirit's voice, discerning what God is revealing and about to do. Elijah's journey shows that if we will withdraw from the noise all around us, we can hear and behold the glory of the Lord. May we seek God in the silence and stillness, and may we perceive the signs of God's impending blessings for us.

The Upward Climb

Historically, Mount Carmel has been the site of many spiritual encounters and divine revelations. The name of the place, "derived from the Hebrew *kerem* (vineyard/garden)" and *el* (God),[4] suggests a place of divine beauty and fertility.[5] This mountainous area in northern Israel is a geographical landmark and a symbol of God's provision and presence.

"So Ahab went up to eat and to drink. Elijah went up to the top of Carmel; there he bowed himself down upon the earth and put his face between his knees" (1 Kings 18:42). Elijah's physical ascent to Carmel's summit is also a sign of spiritual ascent. The Celts speak of "thin places,"[6] locations where the veil between the material and spiritual realms is particularly thin and permeable, allowing for a profound sense of the divine presence and moments of penetrating spiritual insight and transformation. Seeing Mount Carmel as a "thin place," we can explore its significance in a new light.

Up and Down, To and Fro

Mount Carmel typifies the sacred spaces in our lives where the heavenly and the earthly intersect. We can liken this to Christ as the fulfillment of Jacob's ladder. There is movement in our journey, an ascending and descending in relation to spiritual renewal and sustenance that stands in contrast with the "to and fro" of daily existence by which our lives often seem limited.

In the book of Job, God asked the accuser, "Where have you come from?" (Job 1:7). The accuser responded, "From going to and fro on the earth, and from walking up and down on it" (Job 1:7). This phrase reflects the deliberate, vigilant movement of the adversary, who observes and tests human affairs. Similarly, in Daniel 12:4, the increase of knowledge is associated with people running "back and forth," to and fro, symbolizing the state of restless anxiety so often evident in human pursuits.

Christ, however, descends into our earthly existence to make possible our transcending of "to and fro" patterns. He offers instead spiritual ascent and descent. Remember what Jesus said to Nathanael. "Very truly, I tell you, you will see heaven opened and the angels of God ascending and descending upon the Son of Man" (John 1:51). Christ is the fulfillment of Jacob's ladder, symbolizing the reconciliation of heaven and earth in Him. Therefore, our individual journeys can rise above mere existence and become pathways of spiritual renewal and sustenance.

Elijah's climb up Mount Carmel was a spiritual journey toward divine intimacy and understanding. He moved toward the summit where heaven and earth meet, and when he reached it, a clear view of the horizon and the vast Mediterranean Sea opened up. The summit was more than a peak; it was a spiritual and prophetic vantage point where clarity, vision, and divine perspective converged.

Acute Hearing Leads to the Summit

Elijah journeyed to the summit to pray, revealing how faith operates within us, particularly in the space between the "now" and the "not yet." He had already experienced a prophetic hearing of a future reality (rain). Keenly aware and deeply immersed in the hearing of faith, Elijah's attention intensified his agreement with what wanted to emerge. Notice his prophetic hearing did not begin at Carmel's summit; it began lower down the mountain, and it inspired him to move higher.

Elijah's acute hearing at the lower levels of the mountain shows that faith does not demand the full picture in order to believe. Faith begins in the depths of our everyday experiences, in places from which we don't yet see evidence of the promise being fulfilled. But we are called to listen and trust in what God is revealing. Elijah's journey to the summit was fueled by the certainty of God's voice, which began with the quiet assurance that He was at work.

Our spiritual ascent begins when we tune our ears to the sound of God's promises. The faith that inspires us to climb higher comes from intimate communion with God in the lower, not-so-thin places of our lives. In these humble, often hidden moments, we receive the divine impulse to step higher. With each step, our perspective shifts, and God's vision and purposes come into clear view. Our upward movement leads us into an ever-deepening trust in God, the Rock whose way is perfect (Deuteronomy 32:4).

When we pray "Thy kingdom come," the sound we perceive in our spiritual ears becomes more real than what we hear all around us. Faith comes by *that kind* of hearing. It doesn't come by self-effort but by a quality of attention that listens for the Spirit's witness in the present moment. Our attentiveness to God's presence, promises, and voice keeps us watching the Holy Spirit's movements. Day by day, His divine whispers and motions guide, comfort, and challenge us. This active, expectant listening requires not striving but a receptive posture that welcomes what God reveals so we can be aligned with His will.

Elijah's Posture of Faith

Elijah's example teaches us to enter the sacred space of "future now." As he "bowed himself down upon the earth and put his face between his knees" (1 Kings 18:42), his posture facilitated

Is It Rain That I Hear?

this entrance. It might seem an awkward position for prayer. Some compare it to the ancient Near Eastern birthing position, although historical resources to confirm this are scant. Regardless, Elijah's posture is symbolic of humility, intensity, and total immersion in the act of prophetic intercession. His posture's very obliqueness was perhaps part of its prophetic significance.

Elijah's posture was both physical and spiritual. By bowing low, he symbolically acknowledged his dependence on God. This act of humility, combined with his keen hearing of the future rain, encapsulated the essence of prophetic prayer. But notice that Elijah's ascent into this sacred space also required him to lay aside life's distractions. Immersed in the hearing of faith, he was free to pray for the future's inbreaking.

Elijah's posture reflected a radical hope rooted in the certainty that God is faithful. Our posture can do the same. Just as Elijah became attuned to the sound of rushing rain before a single cloud appeared in the sky, we can prepare to hear the sound of God's kingdom advancing. Then we will experience the power of the Spirit, who brings the future into the now.

The Unknown Servant

Suddenly, and without any previous mention, Elijah's personal servant appears in the narrative. His unexplained presence has been a source of speculation among biblical scholars. Some suggest the servant might be Obadiah, the official in King Ahab's court who hid prophets from Jezebel's purge. This view is not common but worth noting given Obadiah's interaction with Elijah earlier in the story. A more widely accepted view does not seek to name the servant but simply accepts him as a helper to Elijah.

If we consider the servant's abrupt appearance in terms of what it might signify, a rich avenue for interpretation opens in relation to listening deeply to the inner witness of the Spirit, discerning wisely so we can make appropriate decisions, and moving forward. Because the servant ran back and forth to check for signs of rain, we know his role was practical. His sudden appearance could symbolize the broader structure of Old Testament prophetic ministry. Prophets often had disciples or attendants, indicating their ministry was not solitary but involved a community. The servant's appearance underscores the legitimacy and authority of Elijah's role as a prophet and can signify the support that prophets' work received within the prophetic tradition. And what is true for all is true for prophets; it is not good for them to be alone (Genesis 2:18).

Sacred Anticipation

From a semiotic standpoint, the unnamed servant draws us into the dramatic tension of what was waiting to unfold. The story's intensity becomes evident when Elijah says to his servant, "Go up now, look toward the sea." We cannot help but anticipate the servant's report. But when he went up and looked he said, "There is nothing." Then Elijah said, "Go again seven times" (1 Kings 18:43).

Seven times! The instruction for the servant to keep going and report back each time represents a ritual of anticipation. This important habit in the journey of faith helps us establish healthy practices and routines in periods of waiting for God's promise to be fulfilled. Just as Elijah's servant checked and rechecked for signs of rain, we can perform daily routines that maintain our focus and momentum. In my view, this means setting aside time each day for journaling, prayer, and meditation on Scripture. In those moments, we can reflect on our pursuits in faith, and we can reaffirm our hopes. Much as the servant's repeated journeys to the sea reinforced his faith, these gestures reinforce ours.

This is not repetition for repetition's sake but rather a way of learning to maintain hope and persistence while avoiding the passivity that expects God to do our part. With awe and reverence, we

Is It Rain That I Hear?

are to work out what God is working in us (Philippians 2:12–13). He will do His part but not ours. For us, then, faith is more than a fact; it is also an act, and the difference is in the doing!

It is not easy to maintain hope amid uncertainty. Yet our sacred rituals are often most powerful in the most challenging moments. Through them, the Spirit can strengthen our resolve and keep us in sync with the aspirations God breathes into us. Consider the simple but powerful act of bringing His promises to speech. Meditating on Scripture means muttering certain texts to ourselves so that when we speak to others, those promises move from our hearts and through our understanding.[7] This process ultimately causes us to speak about what God is doing in us. Thus, these repetitive acts keep our spirits lifted and our focus sharp, as they did for Elijah's servant.

An old adage says, "If you pray for patience, expect troubles." The element of truth in that saying might make you chuckle, but it can also put a knot in your stomach. Nevertheless, learning to cultivate patience and trust is vital. James makes that clear, saying, "My brethren, count it all joy when you fall into various trials" (James 1:2 NKJV). In verse 3, James goes on to say "that the testing of your faith produces patience." So there is good reason to "count it all joy"!

There is another lesson we can learn about sacred anticipation. Elijah's servant reminds us to draw strength from companions. Elijah was a man of faith, but he also drew faith from what his servant began to see. Perhaps prayer partners are out of vogue today, but when I am pressing by faith into an arena I believe God is showing me, I inform a few trusted friends who know me well and have passionate prayer lives. After fifty years of active ministry, I still check in with those I consider mentors and friends. Why? Because they provide external validation and support that helps me stay the course. They love me enough to share my hopes and dreams, and I do the same for them. They remind me that I am part of a larger story.

Take an inventory of your history in God, and you will see how your patience has been tried and fortified in life's waiting periods. Practicing persistence is a way of counting it all joy. Praying the Scriptures back to God reminds you of what He promised and helps you to cultivate a serene and trusting heart. You can do this in your prayer closet or during a prayer walk, for example. Praying amid God's good creation can open a mental space in which you learn to wait with grace. Like Elijah, you can find peace in the waiting, trusting that God's timing is perfect.

Engaging in your own sacred rituals of anticipation will bless and benefit you. The structure and routine these rituals provide will comfort you and offer a sense of balance while helping you to build emotional resilience. These rituals will nurture your faith, reinforce your belief in God's promises, and deepen your trust in His Word and ways. Let them strengthen your bonds with people who will partner with you and remind you that you are not alone in your waiting.

Breakthrough at the Breakpoint

Elijah was well-seasoned in prayer and exemplified what it means to be importunate—a term that brings the parable of the widow and the unjust judge to mind (Luke 18:1–8). The widow relentlessly pursued justice and did it without a beggar's mindset. Her posture illustrates the importunate prayer of believers who come boldly before the throne of grace, confident in God's promise (Hebrews 4:16).

Elijah was both persistent and confident. "At the seventh time [Elijah's servant] said, 'Look, a little cloud no bigger than a person's hand is rising out of the sea'" (1 Kings 18:44). Elijah's persistence served as a catalyst for breakthrough. Despite the servant's repeated reports of seeing nothing, Elijah did not waver. He knew what God had spoken would come to pass. His steadfastness challenges me to be innovative and consistent in my pursuit of God's promises, refusing to quit even when their fulfillment seems delayed.

Elijah's journey of prayer was not primarily about repetitive actions but about a deepening conviction that God would fulfill what He revealed. The journey of faith and prayer includes a breakpoint—a critical moment of decision and action that leads to a significant change or breakthrough. We see such a moment in 1 Chronicles 14, when the God of the Breakthrough (in Hebrew, *Baal-perazim*)[8] prevailed at Baal-perazim, the place of breakthrough. David noted the divine role and his own, saying, "God has broken through my enemies by my hand like a breakthrough of water" (1 Chronicles 14:11 NKJV). By faith, David acted, and one of many possible futures (each built into the creation by the Creator) unfolded.

Elijah also acted by faith and pursued his breakpoint. This pursuit required persistence and the refusal to accept as final the servant's answer of "Nothing." The servant went back seven times to check for rain, symbolizing a perfecting process and deepening of conviction. Elijah was innovative in his faith journey; he kept challenging the drought's seeming status quo by praying and perceiving beyond the visible circumstances. He did more than think outside the box; he prayed outside the box. He did not resign himself to the seeming withholding of rain. Instead, he aligned himself with the God who declares, "I am about to do a new thing; now it springs forth, do you not perceive it?" (Isaiah 43:19).

Prophetic perception allowed Elijah to see possibilities other than drought. He understood spiritual growth not only is linear and incremental but also involves sudden leaps and breakthroughs from thirtyfold, to sixtyfold, and a hundredfold (Mark 4:8). Quantum leaps occur when we persist and witness positive shifts that seem unexpected. When Elijah heard the sound of rushing rain, he knew the breakpoint was near. Based on his inner conviction, he sent the servant back again and again.

The servant's cooperation, adaptability, and flexibility were also crucial. He was willing to pivot and oscillate between the "now" and the "not yet." His repeated trips to the ridge overlooking the sea illustrate his dynamic flow between what is and what is to come. Within this creative tension, he knew what he was looking for, and he wouldn't quit until he saw what Elijah heard. This tells me he accepted Elijah's hearing of the rain as an accomplished reality. It was just a matter of the natural water cycle kicking in.

Remember, Elijah's hearing was connected to his prayer. The prayer of faith sparked innovation, both for him and for his servant. This shows that when we persist in prayer, we challenge the status quo and associate ourselves with God's promises. The breakthroughs that follow then transform our reality. Our part is to remain steadfast and innovative, continually looking for the breakthrough God has promised. Then the fulfillment of His Word can turn our droughts into seasons of abundant rain.

Elijah the Meteorologist

Elijah's prayer revealed his partnership with God in triggering the natural water cycle that begins in the ocean. Understanding this cycle can draw meaningful parallels between natural processes and divine promises. The water cycle describes the continuous, crucial movement of water on, above, and below the surface of the earth. By praying persistently for rain, Elijah participated in a divine process that aligned with the natural, created order.

The cycle begins when the sun's heat causes water to evaporate from the ocean's surface. As the vapor rises, it encounters cooler air at higher altitudes and condenses into tiny droplets that cluster together and form clouds.[9] When the air within the clouds cools to the dew point—the temperature at which air becomes saturated with moisture[10]—the water droplets combine to form larger droplets. When these droplets get heavy enough, they fall to the ground as rain.

Elijah's faith-filled anticipation and repeated actions were like water's evaporation stage, rising to meet God's promise. The servant's seven trips can symbolize the condensation and cloud-formation stages, each trip building the expectancy and aligning with the process. Finally, the sight of the small cloud marked the dew point at which God's promised rain was about to fall. Elijah's faith aligned with the natural process that fulfilled a divine promise.

Applying the Water Process

So how do we apply this process to our lives? We mirror it by engaging in persistent prayer and cooperation with God. Our prayers rise like vapor, full of faith and expectancy. Even when we do not see immediate results, we trust God is forming the "clouds" of His promises. Each step brings us closer to the dew point, where the breakthrough we seek is realized. Just as warm air rises and meets the cooler air to form clouds, our fervent prayers ascend to meet God's divine timing and purpose. When the time is right, the heavens open, and the deluge of blessings pours out.

If ever we needed to pray with Elijah's importunate spirit, it is now! Let's yield to the wisdom and power of the God who continually says, "Let there be," knowing "it is he who made the earth by his power, who established the world by his wisdom, and by his understanding stretched out the heavens" (Jeremiah 51:15).

Significance of the Seventh Time

At the seventh time, the servant saw a cloud as small as a man's hand rising from the sea. This marked the culmination of Elijah's importunate prayer and the divine breakpoint through which rain would come from heaven. The tiny cloud was a monumental sign of what Elijah had put his hand to—not only in prayer but also in the power of the Sovereign Spirit.

Elijah co-labored with God, and at the seventh time, the tangible results became evident. God's hand turned the sign into substance. The breakthrough at the breakpoint involved human effort, but the miracle occurred when God's hand moved in ways human hands could not. Elijah set the stage with his prayers, but God's hand opened the curtain and delivered on His promise.

Remember that the deluge transforms our drought into abundance, but it always testifies to God's work. Yes, we need to continue to encourage ourselves in the Lord (1 Samuel 30:6 KJV). The small cloud reminds us God is working. When He moves, He adds His hand to ours and brings forth the breakthrough.

The Race to Jezreel: A Supernatural Breakthrough

Once the small cloud appeared, a race to Jezreel ensued. Elijah's orders to Ahab were "Harness your chariot and go down [to Jezreel] before the rain stops you" (1 Kings 18:44). In other words, "Rain is on the way, Ahab, so get going!" What happened next is the stuff of Israel's long history. "The heavens grew black with clouds and wind; there was a heavy rain. Ahab rode off and went to Jezreel. But the hand of the LORD was on Elijah; he girded up his loins and ran in front of Ahab to the entrance of Jezreel" (vv. 45–46). Elijah ran at supernatural speed and passed the king's chariot. His display of physical prowess was a potent sign of divine empowerment and prophetic breakthrough.

Jezreel also holds semiotic significance in the biblical narrative. A root of the name *Jezreel* "refers to the action of sowing seed" and can metaphorically denote "the Lord's sowing (planting or establishing)" as in the case of "Israel in the land of Palestine."[11] The word speaks of a place where God's actions and promises come to fruition.

Significant events in Jezreel shaped Israel's history and destiny. Historically, it was a site of judgment and restoration.

God's judgment against the house of Ahab would be executed there. But the place, with its fertile and expansive valley, also symbolized Israel's renewal and restoration. It spoke to the people of new beginnings and the fulfillment of divine promises.

Elijah clearly operated under divine anointing as he outran Ahab's chariot and arrived at Jezreel ahead of the king. This was a triumph of divine sovereignty over human power and royal decrees. When God's Spirit moves, natural laws and limitations yield. But Elijah's girding up of his loins indicates his own readiness and determination. He prepared himself to move swiftly, suggesting the readiness we must adopt when we cooperate with God's purposes. That is when the Spirit enables us to move at the speed of breakthrough, overtaking obstacles and natural limitations that cannot be mastered by human strength.

Elijah's arrival at Jezreel ahead of Ahab illustrates the prophetic fulfillment of God's word. Just as Elijah's prayers triggered the cycle that brought rain, his supernatural run to Jezreel signified the arrival of God's promises at the appointed time.

Lessons for Our Journey

Perhaps the overarching lesson from 1 Kings 18:41–46 is that our yielding to God's will and our persistence in faith divinely empower us to achieve what is otherwise impossible. Like Elijah, we must gird up our loins so we can act as soon as God moves. This level of preparation requires us to be determined. Then we can take full advantage of the opportunities God presents and be in sync with His timing.

Elijah's supernatural run to Jezreel emphasizes God's triumph over human power. It reminds us His plans are sovereign, and His promises will come to pass. The impossible speed and endurance of Elijah's feat also encourage us to persist in prayer and action, trusting that God will bring us to our "Jezreel"— our place of fulfillment and new beginnings.

As we reflect on Elijah's journey, may the Spirit breathe into us the motivation to embrace that which God desires to unfold in our midst. If we persist in prayer—not with slavish groveling but with the boldness of adopted sons and daughters coming to the throne of grace—we ready ourselves for action. And as we trust the Spirit's empowering presence, we too can overtake obstacles and arrive at the place where God's promises are fulfilled.

I believe a clarion call is coming to Jesus' followers in this season. It is a call to embrace the significance of Jezreel, a place where God sows, where His judgment and renewal intersect, and where His divine purposes come to fruition.

Soul-Searching Questions

- When God makes His intentions clear, how can you cultivate the same unwavering determination and persistence in prayer that Elijah displayed? What spiritual disciplines or practices can help you to remain steadfast in intercession, even when the answer seems delayed, or the circumstances appear unchanged?

- In the face of repeated disappointments or setbacks, how can you maintain your faith and continue to pray until the breakthrough comes? What Scripture passages, promises, or past experiences of God's faithfulness can you draw upon to strengthen your resolve and trust in God's perfect timing?

- How can you discern when God is inviting you to travail in prayer for a specific purpose or promise? What might this partnering with God look like? How might it stretch you or take you beyond what seems "usual"? How will you conform to God's invitation rather than expect His invitation to conform to your expectations?

NOT-SO-FINAL THOUGHTS

The triumph at Mount Carmel was stunning, and Elijah's supernaturally swift arrival at Jezreel made God's empowering Spirit evident to all. Yet these events did not guarantee Elijah's future security. The end of the drought did not conclude his conflict with Ahab and Jezebel. It simply set the stage for future challenges.

Mount Carmel was a high point in Elijah's ministry, a moment of undeniable victory that demonstrated Yahweh's power before Ahab, the people of Israel, and the prophets of Baal and Asherah. What Elijah did not anticipate was the fierce pushback Jezebel would undertake (1 Kings 19:2). Her death threat gripped Elijah with a fear so intense and unexpected it drove him to flee. This about-face—from a sense of triumph to one of sheer terror—should humble us all and remind us that even huge victories cannot shield us from future trials.

Elijah's flight began a new season of isolation marked by severe psychological and emotional turmoil. Not long after the stellar showdown on Mount Carmel, God's prophet found himself in despair, feeling utterly alone and even abandoned. This period of deep distress produced a physical journey and Elijah's deep dive into his own soul. By God's grace, this internal

Not-So-Final Thoughts

quest prompted him to grow in ways he had not anticipated or consciously experienced in the past.

During this dark period, God met Elijah and shattered his long-held expectations in relation to his own history and destiny. It is in this chapter of his life that God came in condescending love to accommodate a journey Elijah was not compelled but determined to take. From the heights of Carmel in the Northern Kingdom to the depths of a broom tree in the far desert of the Southern Kingdom, the prophet entered a long day's journey into the dark night of his own soul.

Stay tuned for that story and more! Elijah's trek from the broom tree to a dark cave on Mount Horeb will keep him hiding and hoping to pass from the scene without anyone noticing his end. Instead, he will discover he still has a future, and an emerging generation needs to glean from his prophetic consciousness, perception, wisdom, and power. His turnaround will come as a now reluctant prophet is brought face-to-face with a man called Elisha in the territory of Issachar.

Elijah's journey is far from over, and Elisha's is about to begin. What happens is not only compelling but transformative for them and for us. So let's pick up where we are leaving off now and see what God will do in us along the way!

ACKNOWLEDGMENTS

Every book is a journey, and this one has been no different. I am deeply grateful to those who have made this journey possible and meaningful.

To my wife, Ruth, thank you for once again surrendering precious time together so that I could commit myself to this project. Your love and understanding are the foundation upon which all of my work is built.

Misty Hood, your meticulous management of my schedule created the space I needed to write, even when the demands were high. Your efficiency and care are a gift that brings structure to my otherwise hectic days.

Donna Scuderi, thank you for tirelessly refining my words and shaping them into something palatable. Your attention to detail and willingness to dig deep make all the difference, and I am grateful for your unwavering support.

Kathleen Groom, I am especially grateful for your readiness to undertake the final edit and for scrutinizing every detail with precision. Your thoroughness has ensured that everything in these pages is as it should be.

Finally, Kim Bangs, thank you for your confidence in me and for offering me another chance to work within the cadre

Acknowledgments

of Chosen authors. Your belief in my work continues to be a source of inspiration and encouragement.

To each of you, my heartfelt thanks for your contributions to this work. Without your commitment and care, this book would not have been possible.

NOTES

Introduction

1. Jaroslav Pelikan, *The Vindication of Tradition* (Yale University Press, 1984), 65.

2. Chuck Girard, "Slow Down," Msi Music Administration o/b/o Sea of Glass Music.

3. "Survey Data Confirm Increases in Anxiety, Depression and Suicidal Thinking Among U.S. Adolescents," Johns Hopkins Bloomberg School of Public Health, accessed April 25, 2024, https://publichealth.jhu.edu/2020/survey-data-confirm-increases-in-anxiety-depression-and-suicidal-thinking-among-u-s-adolescents.

4. Johns Hopkins, "Survey Data Confirm Increases."

5. Lantie Elisabeth Jorandby, "Depression and Anxiety Are on the Rise Globally," *Psychology Today*, November 1, 2021, https://www.psychologytoday.com/intl/blog/use-your-brain/202111/depression-and-anxiety-are-the-rise-globally.

6. Jorandby, "Depression and Anxiety Are on the Rise Globally."

7. Zara Abrams, "Student Mental Health Is in Crisis. Campuses Are Rethinking Their Approach," American Psychological Association, last updated October 12, 2022, https://www.apa.org/monitor/2022/10/mental-health-campus-care.

8. Abrams, "Student Mental Health Is in Crisis."

9. "Mental Illness," National Institute of Mental Health, accessed May 22, 2024, https://www.nimh.nih.gov/health/statistics/mental-illness.

Chapter 1 Knowing Where We Come From

1. Max Weber, "Science as a Vocation," 1918, Munich University, transcript, accessed May 22, 2024, https://www.wisdom.weizmann.ac.il/~oded/X/WeberScienceVocation.pdf.

Notes

2. "Of course, science in helping to disenchant the universe, contributed to opening the way for exclusive humanism. A crucial condition for this was a new sense of the self and its place in the cosmos: not open and porous and vulnerable to a world of spirits and powers, but what I want to call 'buffered.'" Charles Taylor, *A Secular Age* (Belknap Press, 2007), 39 (see also 47–54, 73, 95, 312, 551, 793, 867).

3. "Porous . . . having pores; poriferous 3 easy to cross or penetrate . . . from Medieval Latin *porōsus*, from Late Latin *porus* > porously *adv* > porousness *n*." *Collins English Dictionary* (HarperCollins, 2006), under "porous."

4. Taylor, *Secular Age*, 39.

5. "Introduction to Buffers," LibreTexts Chemistry, accessed April 26, 2024, https://chem.libretexts.org/Bookshelves/Physical_and_Theoretical_Chemistry_Textbook_Maps/Supplemental_Modules_(Physical_and_Theoretical_Chemistry)/Acids_and_Bases/Buffers/Introduction_to_Buffers.

6. "חָזוֹן *ḥā·zón a divine vision* [*"a vision*, spoken of a divine vision or dream, Isa. 29:7; specially a vision from God respecting future events, prophetic vision, Lam. 2:9; Micah 3:6; Ps. 89:20"], Dan. 1:17; 8:1; 9:24. Hence—(2) generally a divine *revelation*, 1 Sa. 3:1; 1 Ch. 17:15; Prov. 29:18. (3) *an oracle*, often collectively (compare ὅραμα, Acts 12:5; 16:9), Isa. 1:1; Obad. 1; Nah. 1:1." Wilhelm Gesenius and Samuel Prideaux Tregelles, *Gesenius' Hebrew and Chaldee Lexicon to the Old Testament Scriptures* (Logos Bible Software, 2003), under "חָזוֹן."

7. "(*pā·ra'*): be out of control . . . (Ex 32:25b+); . . . be running wild (Ex 32:25a+); . . . be unrestrained, be lawless (Pr 29:18+); . . . cause disorder, promote wickedness (2Ch 28:19+)." James Swanson, *Dictionary of Biblical Languages with Semantic Domains:Hebrew (Old Testament)* (Logos Research Systems, 1997), under "פָּרַע."

8. Abraham Heschel, "Pathos and Prophecy," *Clarion*, July 1, 2008, https://www.clarion-journal.com/clarion_journal_of_spirit/2008/07/pathos-and-prop.html.

9. William James, *The Principles of Psychology* (Dover Publications, 1890, 1918), 1:233.

10. James, *Principles of Psychology*, 233.

11. Michael J. Gorman, *Cruciformity: Paul's Narrative Spirituality of the Cross* (William B. Eerdmans, 2001), 28.

12. Norman Lamm, *The Shema: Spirituality and Law in Judaism* (Jewish Publication Society, 1998), 13.

Chapter 2 Elijah the Larger-Than-Life Prophet

1. Dan P. McAdams and Kate C. McClean, "Narrative Identity," *Current Directions in Psychological Science* 22, no. 3 (June 2013): 233.

2. Elisabeth A. Nesbit Sbanotto, Heather Davediuk Gingrich, and Fred C. Gingrich, *Skills for Effective Counseling: A Faith-Based Integration* (IVP Academic, 2016), 207–208.

Notes

3. Walter Brueggemann, *The Prophetic Imagination*, 2nd ed. (Fortress Press, 2001), 1.

4. Brueggemann, *The Prophetic Imagination*, 1.

5. Brueggemann, *The Prophetic Imagination*, 1–2.

6. Brueggemann, *The Prophetic Imagination*, 1–2.

Chapter 3 Journeying with Elijah: The Tishbite and His Call

1. Joseph Coleson, "Joshua," in *Cornerstone Biblical Commentary: Joshua, Judges, Ruth*, ed. Philip W. Comfort, Cornerstone Biblical Commentary (Tyndale, 2012), 28–29.

2. "Magical thinking: the belief that events or the behavior of others can be influenced by one's thoughts, wishes, or rituals. Magical thinking is typical of children up to 4 or 5 years of age, after which reality thinking begins to predominate." *APA Dictionary of Psychology*, "magical thinking," accessed May 22, 2024, https://dictionary.apa.org/magical-thinking.

3. Roger Stronstad, *The Prophethood of All Believers: A Study in Luke's Charismatic Theology* (CPT Press, 2010).

4. T. Austin Sparks, "Prophetic Ministry: Chapter 1—What Prophetic Ministry Is," accessed May 22, 2024, https://www.austin-sparks.net/english/books/001003.html.

5. The Torah was part of the written commandment and was probably committed to memory by Hebrew children. It was certainly widespread among the faithful as the oral tradition.

6. T. M. Derico, "Oral Tradition," in *The Lexham Bible Dictionary*, ed. John D. Barry, David Bomar, Derek R. Brown, and Rachel Klippenstein (Lexham Press, 2016), Logos Bible Software 9.

7. Derico, "Oral Tradition," in *Lexham Bible Dictionary*.

8. "Speech Acts," in *Stanford Encyclopedia of Philosophy*, ed. Edward N. Zalta, Fall 2021, accessed May 22, 2024, https://plato.stanford.edu/entries/speech-acts/.

9. Richard Nordquist, "Locutionary Act Definition in Speech-Act Theory," ThoughtCo, last updated July 18, 2019, https://www.thoughtco.com/locutionary-act-speech-1691257t.

10. Nordquist, "Locutionary Act Definition."

11. Nordquist, "Locutionary Act Definition."

Chapter 4 Look What the Wind Blew In (to Ahab's Court)

1. John H. Walton, ed., *Zondervan Illustrated Bible Backgrounds Commentary: Old Testament*, vol. 3, *1 & 2 Kings, 1 & 2 Chronicles, Ezra, Nehemiah, Esther* (Zondervan, 2009), 74.

2. "The eastern seaboard of the Mediterranean receives rainfall from the weakening winter storms of central Europe as they reach the coast of the Holy Land. Drought occurs when the dry season extends well beyond its natural cycle of April through September. . . . The catastrophic nature of

Notes

this drought is seen in the absence of dew, which is vital to vineyards and trees during the dry summer months." Walton, *Zondervan Illustrated Bible Backgrounds Commentary*, 73–74.

3. C. S. Lewis, *The Lion, the Witch and the Wardrobe* (HarperCollins, 2013), 217, 289, Kindle. *The Lion, the Witch and the Wardrobe* by C.S. Lewis copyright © 1950 C.S. Lewis Pte. Ltd. Extract reprinted by permission.

Chapter 5 Knowing Where We're Going

1. Karl-Heinz Bernhardt, Jan Bergman, and Helmer Ringgren, "הָיָה," in *Theological Dictionary of the Old Testament*, ed. G. Johannes Botterweck, trans. David E. Green (William B. Eerdmans, 1978), 379.

2. Bernhardt et al., *Theological Dictionary*, 379.

3. This preparation is similar to that of young Samuel, who was also initiated into the sacred experience of hearing from God (1 Samuel 3:1–3). Those called into God's council, as described in the prophetic traditions of the Mosaic law and the prophets, were endowed with the ability to discern the unique voice and word of God.

4. Daniel J. Brendsel, *Answering Speech: The Life of Prayer as Response to God* (Crossway, 2023), 18, Kindle.

5. Eugene H. Peterson, *Working the Angles: The Shape of Pastoral Integrity* (William B. Eerdmans, 1987), 45.

6. Brendsel, *Answering Speech*, 18.

7. W. S. LaSor, "Cherith," in *The International Standard Bible Encyclopedia*, rev. ed., ed. Geoffrey W. Bromiley (William B. Eerdmans, 1979–1988), 641; Walter A. Elwell and Barry J. Beitzel, *Baker Encyclopedia of the Bible*, under "Cherith, The Brook" (Baker, 1988), 428; "Cherith, Brook of," in *Lexham Bible Dictionary*.

8. Gesenius and Tregelles, *Hebrew and Chaldee Lexicon*, under "כְּרִית."

9. "Cherith Meaning," Abarim Publications, accessed May 18, 2024, https://www.abarim-publications.com/Meaning/Cherith.html.

10. Jennie Wilson, "Hold to God's Unchanging Hand," in *African American Heritage Hymnal 404* (GIA Publications, 2000).

11. New American Standard Bible (Lockman Foundation, 1995), Ps. 46:1, n[b] and n[c], accessed May 18, 2024, https://www.biblegateway.com/passage/?search=ps+46&version=NASB1995.

12. William James, *The Principles of Psychology* (Dover Publications, 1918), 233.

13. *Merriam-Webster*, "spirit," accessed October 17, 2024, https://www.merriam-webster.com/dictionary/spirit.

Chapter 6 Fed by Dirty Birds

1. Examples include: Marcus Buckingham, "The Top 10 Findings on Resilience and Engagement," MIT Sloan Management Review, March 1, 2021, https://sloanreview.mit.edu/article/the-top-10-findings-on-resilience-and-engagement/; Marcus Buckingham, "The Sources of Resilience," MIT Sloan

218

Notes

Management Review, October 27, 2020, https://sloanreview.mit.edu/article/the-sources-of-resilience/; Rob Cross, Karen Dillon, and Danna Greenberg, "The Secret to Building Resilience," *Harvard Business Review*, January 29, 2021, https://hbr.org/2021/01/the-secret-to-building-resilience; Kendra Cherry, "How Resilience Helps You Cope with Life's Challenges," Verywell Mind, last updated May 3, 2023, https://www.verywellmind.com/what-is-resilience-2795059; "What We Get Wrong About Resilience and What the Research Really Says," NeuroLeadership Institute, April 28, 2021, https://neuroleadership.com/your-brain-at-work/resilience-research.

2. *APA Dictionary of Psychology*, "resilience," accessed May 20, 2024, https://dictionary.apa.org/resilience.

3. *APA Dictionary of Psychology*, "resilience."

4. Anaïs Nin, *Seduction of the Minotaur* (Swallow Press, 1969), 124.

5. *APA Dictionary of Psychology*, "coping strategy," https://dictionary.apa.org/coping-strategy; "emotion-focused coping," https://dictionary.apa.org/emotion-focused-coping; "coping behavior," https://dictionary.apa.org/coping-behavior; all accessed May 20, 2024.

6. Walter Brueggemann, *The Prophetic Imagination*, 2nd ed. (Fortress Press, 2001), 26.

Chapter 7 Life in a Culture of Death

1. Maura Sala, "Sidon" in *Lexham Bible Dictionary*.

2. Solomon is believed to have reigned from around 970 to 931 BCE; Ahab's tenure was from approximately 874 to 853 BCE.

3. Maura Sala, "Sidon" in *Lexham Bible Dictionary*.

4. Chet Roden, "Jezebel, Wife of Ahab, Daughter of Ethbaal," in *Lexham Bible Dictionary*.

5. George Santayana, *The Life of Reason or the Phases of Human Progress* (Charles Scribner's Sons, 1905), 284.

6. Santayana, *Life of Reason*, 284.

7. Santayana, *Life of Reason*, 284.

8. Francis Brown, Samuel Rolles Driver, and Charles Augustus Briggs, *Enhanced Brown-Driver-Briggs Hebrew and English Lexicon* (Clarendon Press, 1977), under "צָרַךְ."

Chapter 8 On the Threshold of Flourishing

1. *Merriam-Webster*, "threshold," accessed June 1, 2024, https://www.merriam-webster.com/dictionary/threshold.

2. Corey L. M. Keyes, "The Mental Health Continuum: From Languishing to Flourishing in Life," *Journal of Health and Social Science Research* 43, no. 2 (June 2002): 1, https://www.jstor.org/stable/3090197.

3. Keyes, "Mental Health Continuum."

4. Austin Farrer, *Faith and Speculation: An Essay in Philosophical Theology Containing the Deems Lectures for 1964* (Adam and Charles Black, 1967), 80.

Notes

Chapter 9 Rising out of Dead Things

1. John J. Pilch, "Honor and Shame," Oxford Bibliographies, last modified January 11, 2012, https://www.oxfordbibliographies.com/display/document/obo-9780195393361/obo-9780195393361-0077.xml.

2. Stephen G. Dempster, "Widow," Bible Study Tools, accessed June 3, 2024, https://www.biblestudytools.com/dictionaries/bakers-evangelical-dictionary/widow.html.

3. Dempster, "Widow"; David Ralph Seely and Jo Ann H. Sealy, "The Cry of the Widow, the Fatherless, and the Stranger: The Covenant Obligation to Help the Poor and Oppressed," *Religious Educator* 23, no. 3 (2022): 86–107, https://rsc.byu.edu/vol-23-no-3-2022/cry-widow-fatherless-stranger.

4. "YHWH and Marginalizational: Israel's Widows and Abuelita Theology," CBE International, accessed June 26, 2024, https://www.cbeinternational.org/resource/yhwh-and-marginalization-israels-widows-and/.

5. "The *w* was a foreigner or a stranger coming into the community, someone who was not part of the family-based social structure. Strangers are in a vulnerable position as they travel." Garwood P. Anderson, "Hospitality," in *Lexham Theological Wordbook*, ed. Douglas Mangum et al. (Lexham Press, 2014), Logos Bible Software 10.

6. Katharine Doob Sakenfeld, *Just Wives? Stories of Power and Survival in the Old Testament and Today* (Westminster John Knox Press, 2003), 33. Sakenfeld explores the stories of women in the Old Testament, including the widow of Zarephath, highlighting the challenges and risks they faced in their cultural contexts. She addresses the social vulnerabilities and potential for misunderstandings that women like the widow had to navigate.

7. Mary Joan Winn Leith, "Gender and Religion: Gender and Near Eastern Religions," Encyclopedia.com, accessed June 27, 2024, https://www.encyclopedia.com/environment/encyclopedias-almanacs-transcripts-and-maps/gender-and-religion-gender-and-ancient-near-eastern-religions.

8. Leith, "Gender and Religion."

9. John Gray, *I & II Kings: A Commentary* (Westminster Press, 1970), 381. Gray provides a commentary on the books of Kings, offering insights into the social and cultural context of the narratives. He discusses Elijah's status as a sojourner and the potential social implications of his interactions with the widow.

10. Victor H. Matthews and Don C. Benjamin, "Social Sciences and Biblical Studies," *Semeia* 68 (1995): 10.

11. "Understanding Guilt, Shame, and Fear Cultures, Honor," Shame Resources for Global Ministry, accessed June 3, 2024, https://honorshame.com/understanding-guilt-shame-fear-cultures/.

12. John H. Walton, *Ancient Near Eastern Thought and the Old Testament: Introducing the Conceptual World of the Hebrew Bible* (Baker Academic, 2006), 107–108; Joel Hamme Bryan, C. Babcock, and Justin David Strong, "Hammurabi, Code of," in *Lexham Bible Dictionary*.

Notes

13. Adam McKee and Scott Bransford, "Understanding Scapegoating in Sociology," *Fundamentals of Sociology*, accessed June 27, 2024, https://docmckee.com/oer/soc/sociology-glossary/scapegoating-definition/.

14. *APA Dictionary*, "defense mechanism," https://dictionary.apa.org/defense-mechanism; "projection," https://dictionary.apa.org/projection; both accessed June 27, 2024.

15. Brené Brown, *Atlas of the Heart: Mapping Meaningful Connection and the Language of Human Experience* (Random House, 2021), 137.

16. Brown, *Atlas of the Heart*, 139.

17. Paula S. Hiebert, "'Whence Shall Help Come to Me?' The Biblical Widow," in *Gender and Difference in Ancient Israel*, ed. Peggy L. Day (Fortress Press, 1989), 130.

18. Hiebert, "'Whence Shall Help Come to Me?,'" 130, 137.

19. "In classical psychoanalytic theory and other forms of depth psychology, [repression is] the basic defense mechanism that excludes painful experiences and unacceptable impulses from consciousness." *APA Dictionary*, "repression," accessed June 27, 2024, https://dictionary.apa.org/repression.

20. "[Suppression is] a conscious effort to put disturbing thoughts and experiences out of mind, or to control and inhibit the expression of unacceptable impulses and feelings." *APA Dictionary*, "suppression," accessed June 27, 2024, https://dictionary.apa.org/suppression.

21. "τέλειος, α, ον . . . 'attaining an end or purpose, complete' . . . pert. to meeting the highest standard." William Arndt et al., eds., *A Greek-English Lexicon of the New Testament and Other Early Christian Literature* (University of Chicago Press, 2000), under "τέλειος." "τέλειος *téleios*; fem. *teleía*, neut. *teleion*, adj. from *télos* (5056), goal, purpose. Finished, that which has reached its end, term, limit; hence, complete, full, wanting in nothing." Spiros Zodhiates, *The Complete Word Study Dictionary: New Testament* (AMG Publishers, 2000), under "τέλειος *téleios*."

22. Jonathan Black, "The Incarnation: 'He Became What We Are So That We Might Become What He Is," *Apostolic Theology*, December 4, 2014, https://www.apostolictheology.org/2014/12/the-incarnation-he-became-what-we-are.html.

23. "θρησκεία thrēskeía; . . . from *thrēskeúō* (n.f.), to worship God, which is from *thréskos* (2357), religious, pious. Worshiping or worship. In Col. 2:18, mentions the worship of angels. This is probably a gen. of association and alludes to the false, gnostic doctrine of celestial exaltation in which human worshipers were permitted to share in the worship activities of various grades of angelic beings. It also refers to the true worship of God (Acts 26:5; James 1:26, 27). *Thrēskeía* is contrasted with *theosébeia* (2317), external worship, meaning reverential worship, and *eusébeia* (2150), piety or godliness, and *eulábeia* (2124), devotion arising from godly fear or acceptance of what God directs or permits. *Thrēskeía* may thus refer only to ceremonial service or worship as Paul refers to the religion of the Jews (Acts 26:5). James refers to pure religion (James 1:26, 27), indicating there is also an impure

Notes

religion which would be external worship but not the practice of that which God demands of man." Zodhiates, *Complete Word Study Dictionary*, under "θρησκεία *thrēskeía*."

Chapter 10 The Hour Has Come

1. This Obadiah, who lived in the ninth century before Christ, is not the sixth-century canonical prophet Obadiah, whose short book prophesied the fall of Edom.

Chapter 11 Place Your Bets

1. "'Hinder, beset, treat with hostility, injure.'" R. Mosis, "עָכַר," in *Theological Dictionary of the Old Testament*, ed. G. Johannes Botterweck, Helmer Ringgren, and Heinz-Josef Fabry, trans. David E. Green (William B. Eerdmans, 2001), 69. The same word is used in Proverbs 15:27, when Solomon asserts that greed for unjust gain brings trouble to one's own household. The idea is that selfish motives can have far-reaching consequences for the community. This was the case when Achan hoarded forbidden booty from the battle of Jericho, which resulted in Israel's bitter defeat at Ai.

2. "Carmel means 'garden' or 'vineyard,' referring to the area's fertile beauty." Jeremy D. Otten, "Carmel, Mount," in *Lexham Bible Dictionary*.

3. "שִׂיג: [meaning] bowel movement." William Lee Holladay and Ludwig Köhler, *A Concise Hebrew and Aramaic Lexicon of the Old Testament* (Leiden: Brill, 2000), 350.

Chapter 12 Restoring the Altar of the Lord

1. David Woodruff Smith, "Phenomenology," *Stanford Encyclopedia of Philosophy*, Summer 2018, ed. Edward N. Zalta, https://plato.stanford.edu /entries/phenomenology/.

2. The philosophy of phenomenology was founded by Edmund Husserl in the twentieth century. It is not primarily concerned with preconceived ideas or why experiences happen. Husserl adopted a word from Greek philosophy, *ephoché*, which means "suspension of judgment." The Greek Skeptics used the term to manage their belief that nothing could be known for certain. They suggested that when faced with disagreements or debates, it was best to remain neutral and maintain "peace of mind." *Britannica*, "epoché," accessed June 26, 2024, https://www.britannica.com/topic/epoche.

3. "Epoche," *Britannica*, accessed June 26, 2024, https://www.britannica .com/topic/epoche.

4. "Šāḥaṭ means 'to kill,' most often in a ritual sacrifice and a few times to kill another person(s). . . . In Jer 9:8 [H 7] alone is the lethal weapon the tongue." Victor P. Hamilton, "2362 שָׁחַט," in *Theological Wordbook of the Old Testament*, ed. R. Laird Harris, Gleason L. Archer Jr., and Bruce K. Waltke (Moody Press, 1999), 915.

Notes

5. Walter Brueggemann, *Smyth and Helwys Bible Commentary: 1 and 2 Kings*, ed. Samuel E. Balentine (Smyth & Helwys, 2000), 226.

6. Luke Timothy Johnson, *The Gospel of Luke*, Sacra Pagina, vol. 3 (Liturgical Press, 1991), 347.

Chapter 13 Is It Rain That I Hear?

1. Maggie Ross, *Silence: A User's Guide, Volume Two* (Cascade Books, 2017). Ross notes that true spiritual transformation involves moving from glory to glory through the process of *kenosis* (self-emptying), which allows us to become more attuned to the divine presence.

2. Ross, *Silence*.

3. Ross, *Silence*.

4. *Britannica*, "Mount Carmel," accessed June 24, 2024, https://www.britannica.com/place/Mount-Carmel-mountain-ridge-Israel.

5. Roseanne T. Sullivan, "Carmelites Visit Mount Carmel, Part I," Dappled Things, accessed June 24, 2024, https://www.dappledthings.org/deep-down-things/11968/carmelites-visit-mount-carmel-part-i.

6. "Thin Place," Celtic Glory, accessed June 24, 2024, https://www.celticglory.com/thin-place.

7. Glenna Marshall, "To Know What Is True, Meditate on God's Word," *Revive Our Hearts*, August 15, 2023, https://www.reviveourhearts.com/blog/to-know-what-is-true-meditate-on-gods-word.

8. "Baal-perazim Meaning," Abarim Publications, accessed November 5, 2024, https://www.abarim-publications.com/Meaning/Baal-perazim.html.

9. "The Water Cycle," UCAR Center for Science Education, accessed June 25, 2024, https://scied.ucar.edu/learning-zone/how-weather-works/water-cycle.

10. "Dew Point," Science Direct, accessed June 25, 2024, https://www.sciencedirect.com/topics/engineering/dew-point.

11. Walter C. Kaiser, "582 זָרַע," in *Theological Wordbook of the Old Testament*, 252.

DR. MARK CHIRONNA

is a distinguished leader with a global influence, serving as a prophetic voice for five decades. He is the founder and pastor emeritus of Church on the Living Edge in Longwood, Florida, and the presiding bishop of Legacy Edge Alliance, a worldwide fellowship of senior apostolic leaders and churches. He is also bishop protector of the Order of St. Maximus, a *first of its kind* in the Pentecostal tradition and steeped in the ancient faith. Dr. Chironna holds advanced degrees in theology and psychology, including a master of arts in psychology from Saybrook University, a doctor of ministry in applied semiotics and futures studies from George Fox University, and a doctor of philosophy in Pentecostal theology from the University of Birmingham, UK. He and his wife, Ruth, reside in Orlando, Florida.

Connect with Dr. Mark Chironna:

- MarkChironna.com
- /DrMarkChironna
- @MarkChironna
- @MarkChironna
- @DrMarkChironna
- The Edge Podcast with Dr. Mark Chironna (all streaming platforms)
- MarkChironna.substack.com